Seton Gordon's Cairngorms

Seton Gordon's Cairngorms

AN ANTHOLOGY

Compiled by Hamish Brown

Whittles Publishing

Published by
Whittles Publishing,
Dunbeath,
Caithness KW6 6EY,
Scotland, UK

www.whittlespublishing.com

ISBN 978-1904445-88-3

Printed by InPrint, Latvia

CONTENTS

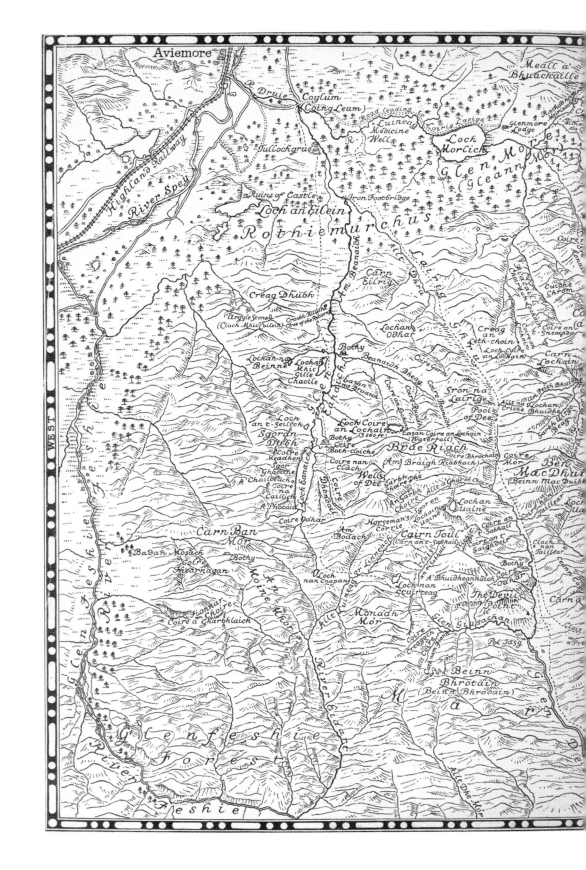

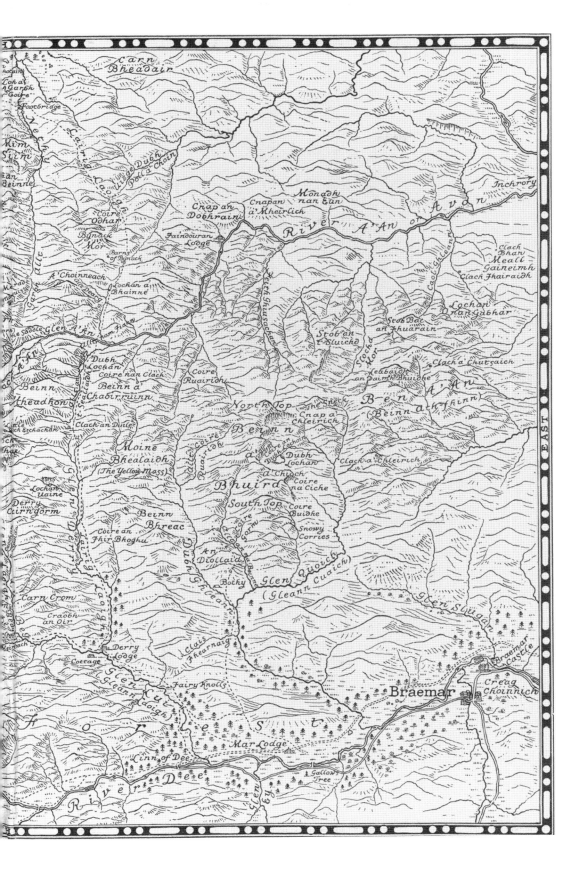

PREFACE

Quite how anyone becomes captivated by wildlife and the outdoors is a mystery but Seton Gordon 'got it early and got it bad'. He obviously had understanding and encouraging parents but, from that well-to-do background, heading off with gun rather than camera would have been the norm. He quietly made himself an extraordinary pioneer during a period ever-harder to envisage. The few figures in his photographs wear garments which long predated synthetic materials. Gordon himself took to wearing a kilt, off or on the hill, in bothy or mansion, careless of its ultimately patched appearance. His early photography was amazing (no putting a digital miniature to a telescope) and many of his earliest pictures were taken simply by stalking his quarry, then shot from cramped hides (he was a tall man) and using weighty and cumbersome primitive cameras. By his teens he was being published and in 1907, at twenty-one years of age, his first book appeared, *Birds of the Loch and Mountain*. In the Preface of that book he gives a description of just what was needed to obtain the early eagle pictures:

> To obtain the photograph of the eyrie a ladder and rope had to be carried up the hill. When this was done it was found that the ladder was not long enough to reach the first branch of the pine tree on which the eyrie was built. Accordingly, when I had climbed as high as possible, the keeper raised the ladder and supported it on his chest, thus adding several feet to its length and enabling me to gain a foothold on the branch, the camera being hauled up afterwards by rope. The photographing of the eyrie was rather risky for the camera was in constant danger of falling and the branch on which I was standing was old and rotten but, luckily, held my weight.

Quite apart from the performance, what other teenager of that period was likely to be given such aid by a keeper?

The young Seton then goes on to describe sitting up all night to record the times when various birds started singing, mentions long hill days and being caught on top of Ben Macdhui in a blizzard. Already knowing the wilds at every season of the year he suggests 'they are at their finest during the month of June, when all Nature at this height looks at her best and the air is laden with the scent of the mountain plants.' The Preface opens with the words:

> I have always had a great love for the solitude and calm of the lone Scottish mountains where a peace and happiness are to be found unknown to the dwellers in the plains. Here one seems to be apart from the sorrows and anxieties of the world and the days I have spent among the ptarmigan and golden plover I shall always remember as the happiest of my experience. What can be more lovely than a mid-winter sunset from a dark lofty mountain, with many a snow wreath lingering on its slopes?

Seton Gordon died just short of his 91st birthday (1886–1977). Even in his later years he continued to discuss and write in much the same manner as he had always; with the same revelational wonder and freshness. He wrote in poetic prose, descriptions only possible by someone intimately at home in the hills with their interacting, connected features: birds, plants, trees, geology, weather, snowbeds, Gaelic culture, place names, history and folklore – an ecologist before the word was coined. (He had graduated in biology with honours, making a special study of the snowbed plants of the Cairngorms.)

He was pre-eminently a naturalist, not a scientist, though his vast knowledge of golden eagles led to two seminal books on eagles and he wrote a great deal on special subjects, such as tree production in the Great War, but which did not appear in book form. He also covered a wide range of journalism, reporting for many years on the Braemar Gathering for instance. He was a piper and a regular judge of piping at various games, another lifelong interest.

Gordon's first article was published when he was fifteen and was soon, I feel sure, set on a career that involved wildlife and writing in one way or another. Early on he acquired cameras, a motorcycle and a car from his parents, who did nothing to discourage him; all were a means to an end. Diaries survive for 1905–1907 when Gordon was leaving his teens in what I suppose were gap years before Oxford. He was out almost every day studying birds, ranging river, loch and moor, climbing Clachnaben, Cairn Taggart, Morven, Lochnagar, and all the little hills of Dee and Don, some many times over. He already had found nests of ptarmigan, golden plover, grouse, curlew and lapwing. He was already noticing snowbeds on the big hills. There was still time, however, for the Lonach Gathering, much golf in the autumn, cricket, fishing, trains and Sunday walks with his father. He rode the engine to Kingussie on one occasion then 'cycled and walked to Braemar' by Glen Feshie and the Geldie. (His railway help during the General Strike in 1926 earned him a medal.) He began to explore Ben A'an, Macdhui and Braeriach, staying with keepers or in bothies. He had his own dark room. Tom Weir in a 1959 interview recorded Gordon saying: 'When I first knew the Cairngorm area Mar Forest was owned by the Duke of Fife whose wife was the Princess Royal, sister of King George V. The duke was an autocrat but he was also the most considerate and helpful if his permission was asked to study and photograph rare birds ... Stalkers were sent with me to carry my half-plate camera and I was always made welcome at their homes.'

He once spent 26 days at the Wells of Dee to establish the incubation period of ptarmigan on the Braeriach plateau. Tom Weir added that Gordon was 'a remarkable character to whom I owed entirely my early interest in birds ... It profoundly influenced my own desire to see these things and write about them when I grew up'. Likewise George Waterston wrote of 'a remarkable character to whom I owed entirely my early interest in birds'. Morton Boyd in his autobiography mentions many people who inspired him when young with 'a passion for knowledge, adventure and spiritual fulfillment as an explorer and naturalist' but added 'Seton Gordon and Fraser Darling, however, gave me a special longing because they spoke to me of my own country which I loved more than any other, and of which as yet I knew so little'.

Gordon's advocate father was the long-serving town clerk of Aberdeen and his mother the unofficial 'Queen's Poetess'. They lived in Aberdeen but had a 'chalet', Auchintoul, at Aboyne. Though well enough off there was the strong work ethic so common in Scotland. Gordon would leave a considerable fortune but was never ostentatiously wealthy. (His second wife, Betty Badger, owned Biddleston Manor, Northamptonshire.) Oxford in the early twentieth century saw him become friends of the then Prince of Wales, the Russian Prince Youssoupoff, Denys Finch-Hatton (a fellow golfing 'half-blue') and some of the great Scottish landowners. Many of them would be swallowed up by demanding duties, but Gordon, too, followed his chosen direction; one that some of his friends no doubt envied. There are letters from Ramsay Macdonald, when Prime Minister, trying to meet up for a stolen walk on a northern visit or inviting Gordon to lunch at No. 10 for a brief respite from the pressures of office. (The PM knew the Cairngorms from long family walks and sleeping out.) I've seen a letter from Prince Philip enclosing a proud photograph of a nest that he took in the Hebrides and Prince Charles as a schoolboy at Gordonstoun wrote regularly to Gordon. When Desmond Nethersole-Thompson and Adam Watson wrote their highly acclaimed *The Cairngorms* (1974) it was dedicated to Gordon, who had inspired both men when they were schoolboys. (When Nethersole-

Thompson wrote the definitive work *The Snow Bunting* he used some of Gordon's pictures of 1909 in it.)

That Seton Gordon started to pioneer the study of wildlife for its own sake, in a world where many landowners and keepers were mainly interested in slaughtering fur and feather, is extraordinary, that he did so in the carefully preserved Cairngorms and won the help of these men is even more extraordinary. He must have been a very special person.

He was one of the first genuinely all-round, exploratory naturalists in Scotland and, if he would no doubt have welcomed today's cameras, I doubt if our narrow, scientific specialisation would have altogether held his lifelong devotion that, in his own words, was a 'fascination which is enhanced by the difficulties to be overcome'. How lucky we are then to have had this prophet, this forerunner, who would inspire and, likewise, enthuse others with his steady flow of writing through the twentieth century. On many expeditions he mentions a companion; this was almost always his first wife, Audrey Pease, met as a student at Oxford, who shared much of their eagle studies and took her share of the photographs that illustrated his books. Both her ashes and Seton's were to be scattered on the Cairngorms.

Grey of Fallodon, the statesman and 'bird' author, was a friend of Gordon and his wife's family in Northumberland, and in a 1924 address to the Royal Society of Literature on 'The Pleasures of Reading' said 'If books about Nature are to live they must be books written as the result of observation, which recall and convert the emotion after it has sunk into the mind. Wordsworth said that poetry was emotion recollected in tranquillity. I think it is true for books on Nature. There should be the result of long observation, much feeling, and tranquility … and brings that sense of leisure and repose for which, in these days, we are more and more grateful'. He could have been describing Gordon.

Seton Gordon, 'the Edwardian gentleman', whose life spanned four reigns, obviously changed very little over the years and, even in the grim days of the Second World War he would write in his 1944 *Highland Year* with ultimate optimism: 'Some people who carry a gun cannot resist slaying anything beautiful or unusual. How blind and incomprehending are these so-called sportsmen. Were they to observe and venerate, their knowledge would be the richer – and not only would they themselves benefit but others would be able to enjoy the same beauty. The war had loosed a flood of hate and misunderstanding yet I do not think that in the future nature lovers will be fewer but rather that they will increase and make their voices heard more and more.'

Gordon wrote two books entirely about the Cairngorms, his first love, the well-known *The Cairngorm Hills of Scotland* (1925) and the earlier *The Charm of the Hills*

(1912) – only his second book – but the Cairngorms would appear in many other titles (even *Islands of the West)* and in a huge range of magazine articles. Most of his books were collections of recycled articles and even before the First World War he was describing 'Red Grouse', 'Cairntoul in Snow', 'At the Haunt of the Eagle' – subjects that never dulled. Most of what appears in this anthology has been culled from books other than *The Cairngorm Hills of Scotland* for later writings had that much more information and experience to draw upon and many also find his earlier *The Charm of the Hills* more engaging.

Writing in *Country Life* in 1976, Gordon recalled his first moment of wildlife interest being stirred by fish. In a Victorian winter with the Dee frozen and the curlers out in force he was enjoying a slide. As his momentum slowed, and before he was caught up by a man and carried onwards, in that one moment, he looked down, between his feet, and through the ice he saw several salmon holding their place against the flow. Oystercatchers were his first bird interest and watching them flying over their Aboyne home with beaks full of worms for their nestlings he wondered how on earth they could still call loud and clear.

His first book was entirely about birds and they would dominate his life as nothing else did, most famously with his studying and writing about golden eagles. So there is quite a large selection one way and another on birds, which I hope fascinates readers, as the birds did the author. What I'm sure will strike readers too is the constant descriptions of heavy winter snows. He would find a quite different pattern today.

Gordon was a prolific writer of both articles and books and, while captivating, the writing could sometimes be hasty, particularly early on where, for instance, the dead adjective 'beautiful' appears three times in two sentences or 'very' seven times in one short chapter. (In reading over this Preface I found I had used the word 'enthusiasm' rather too often, but perhaps that attribute was the key to the success of his writing. Enthusiasm is often contagious.) In many ways, his prose grew more substantial (but still poetic) as the years rolled on. He kept faith with his readers. And I have kept faith in his art. Selections have only been edited to avoid repetitions, standardise layout and punctuation, and prune circumlocutions whether in a word, sentence or paragraph, but the book is still all Seton Gordon. There never was, nor will be, anyone quite like him. Any added comments are given in square brackets [ ] and there are minimal linking passages. Rather than interrupt the flow of the writing, his use of miles and feet has been retained, after all, many heights have gone through several revisions since he wrote and the slight differences are unimportant. Spellings of hill features, and the hills themselves, have changed over the years but I have left these as they appear. I don't think there will be confusion over Brae Riach and Braeriach or Loch A'an and Loch Avon.

I have known the Cairngorms over a lifetime too, have walked the lairigs, climbed and skied in its fastness, visited every Munro at least seven times, been as entranced by dotterel and ptarmigan, relished sun and storm and the very character that makes the Cairngorms different and special. If I could only have one memory it would be of a winter assessment course at Glenmore Lodge when a candidate and I crossed at night from Glen Feshie to reach Braeriach's summit for a bivouac – not my first there either – in a world made glorious by deep snow and a dazzling full moon, an experience it would take the pen of Seton Gordon to describe adequately.

Gordon lived for the first half of his life in the shadow of the Cairngorms, both Deeside and Speyside, and has left a rich legacy in his descriptions of that unique mountain range. (For understanding his greater knowledge of Scotland – he lived in Skye for the second half of his life – see *Seton Gordon's Scotland* (Whittles Publishing, 2005). Because early pictures are now so historic and pictures of Gordon himself tend to be of his later years, there is a tendency to only see the 'grand old man'. I've already mentioned his energetic youthfulness and would simply reiterate that he was a young man when discovering the Cairngorms, and he was a young man when first writing about them. If the quality of the illustrations vary, bear in mind some are over a hundred years old and are included for historical interest, and to show Gordon as the young pioneer. Looking at a picture of his first car gives quite a jolt when one realises the driver would live to see technology take men to the moon.

These selected essays and observations on this special landscape are for dipping into rather than reading straight through. May the selection delight old loyalists and inspire new readers, and may its enthusiasms be reflected in our care for these hills and their precious wildlife.

Hamish M Brown
Burntisland

ACKNOWLEDGEMENTS

As always, the staff of the National Library of Scotland in Edinburgh were most helpful in providing access to the Seton Gordon archive and Sheila Mackenzie organised the scanning of many pictures involved. Other work on the illustration was provided by Tommy Dunbar, Burntisland. James Macdonald Lockhart, as Seton Gordon's literary executor – and grandson – gave support to the project and many friends made suggestions as to what should be included. Adam Watson brought snowfield details up to date and Robin Campbell was able to give me the name of James Gray Kyd (Seton Gordon rarely named 'companions' – usually his wife). Thanks, too, to Dick Balharry for his Foreword. The Cairngorms have had a very special place in many people's lives.

FOREWORD

The area established in 2003 as the Cairngorm National Park covers 3800 km² with prospects for additional areas of the Tilt and Garry river catchments. Thirty-nine per cent of the Park is protected by national, European and international designations. It contains Britain's most extensive arctic alpine habitat and four of Scotland's highest mountains. Its mountain springs, high lochs and lochans, and feeder burns eventually become the rivers Dee and Don flowing to the North Sea at Aberdeen and the river Spey heading to the Moray Firth. Fragments of magnificent ancient Caledonian Forest provide habitats for rare and threatened forest dwellers such as red squirrel, crested tit, capercailzie and industrious wood ants. This remarkable and beautiful area then was the 'calf ground' for the young Seton Gordon, to which he devoted years of his life, his observations and recordings happily still with us in his many books.

A century ago now, in his first book (1907), he wrote: 'The work has to me been a labour of love, and none save those who have actually taken up this branch of National History can have any idea of the fascination it holds for the true lover of Nature – a fascination which is enhanced by the difficulties to be overcome.' This was Seton's workplace, and his wonder for the Cairngorms and interest in all that lived there never waned. His descriptive writing takes you into magical places and his legacy of photographs are testimony to his energy and sense of purpose. Producing high quality work from heavy, awkward equipment he recorded wildlife images that still match modern efforts. In all his books he translated his love, interest and talents to encourage readers to care, respect and value wild country and its wildlife – and the people who lived and worked on it.

His presence as judge at Highland games piping competitions indicates both his own prowess on the music of the Gael and the high esteem given to him by the Highland community. His distinguished kilted figure attracted friendship and support from Royalty, landowners and the people who lived and worked in the landscape from which he drew his inspiration. His highly developed awareness of the mountain world and the resulting first hand accounts appealed to a wide readership. Other highly accomplished writers were to follow: Nan Shepherd, Tom Weir, Nethersole-Thompson and W.H. Murray were among many who left a Cairngorm signature. Most prominent in carrying Seton's flame is Adam Watson who was encouraged as a boy by Seton Gordon to continue his pursuit of wild interests and who became the prime advocate ecologist who highlighted the importance of the Cairngorms.

Having shown himself another devotee by producing the excellent compilation *Seton Gordon's Scotland* (2005), Hamish Brown is the ideal author to further the revival of interest in Seton Gordon's writing. Hamish has wandered wild country all his life and has a well-won reputation as mountaineer, writer and photographer. It is timely, relevant and appropriate to remind ourselves of the immense contribution that Seton's writing was to maintaining the interest which would lead to the establishment of the Cairngorms Nature Reserve, which is now at the core of the National Park. The Park is home to 1600 people but attracts about 1.4 million visitors a year. This compilation will benefit many new readers and visitors and instil the desire to admire, wonder and respect, in turn encouraging a new generation prepared to use lungs and limbs and ultimately be guardians of the Cairngorms.

I read *Days with the Golden Eagle* as a boy and was hooked on the writing of Seton Gordon but had to wait until the early 1970s for the privilege of meeting him. Hill walks and talks followed and, although eighty-five, his blue eyes sparkled with passion and enthusiasm as we shared the spectacular sky dances of the golden eagle near his latter home at Duntulm in Skye. His memories were acute and he was ever eager to walk the hill.

Seton Gordon sometimes voiced concern about the pressures of people on the places he loved and feared for their long-term future – Would he have approved of the National Park? – People, however, always had a place in his practical vision and inspiration was matched by education. Above all people could encounter in the Cairngorms a place of rare non-material pleasures. John Muir wrote: 'Thousands of tired, nerve shaken over-civilised people are beginning to find out that going to the mountains is going home; that wildness is a necessity; and that mountain parks and reservations are useful not only as fountains of timber and irrigating rivers, but as fountains of life.' John Muir had to travel thousands of miles to discover that, while Seton Gordon found it on his doorstep – where it lies for us all today.

Dick Balharry

SETON GORDON BIBLIOGRAPHY

Date	Title	Publisher	Abbreviation
1907	Birds of the Loch and Mountain	Cassell	BLM-07
1912	The Charm of the Hills	Cassell	COH-12
1915	Hill Birds of Scotland	Arnold	HBS-15
1920	Land of the Hills and Glens	Cassell	LHG-20
1921	Wanderings of a Naturalist	Cassell	WON-21
1922	Amid Snowy Wastes	Cassell	(Spitsbergen)
1923	Hebridean Memories	Cassell	HM-23
1925	The Cairngorm Hills of Scotland	Cassell	CHS-25
1926	The Immortal Isles	Williams & Norgate	TIL-26
1927	Days with the Golden Eagle	Williams & Norgate	DGE-27
1929	The Charm of Skye	Cassell	COS-29
1931	In the Highlands	Cassell	ITH-31
1933	Islands of the West	Cassell	IOW-33
1935	Highways & Byways in the West Highlands	Macmillan	H&BW-35
1935	Sea-Gulls in London	Cassell	SIL-35
1936	Thirty Years of Nature Photography	Cassell	30Y-36
1937	Afoot in Wild Places	Cassell	AWP-37
1937	Edward Grey and His Birds	Country Life	EG-37
1938	Wild Birds of Britain	Batsford	WBB-38
1941	In Search of Northern Birds	Eyre & Spottiswoode	ISNB-41

1944	A Highland Year	Eyre & Spottiswoode	HY-44
1948	Highways & Byways in the Central Highlands	Macmillan	H&BC-48
1950	Afoot in the Hebrides	Country Life	AH-50
1951	The Highlands of Scotland	Hale	HOS-51
1955	The Golden Eagle, King of Birds	Collins	GE-55
1963	Highland Days	Cassell	HD-63
1971	Highland Summer	Cassell	HS-71

The Isle of Skye [c.1935]. A 3opp well-illustrated booklet, published in Aberdeen, much on history, Flora Macdonald, etc. Scarce!

Seton Gordon also wrote many sections of, or introductions to, guide books/picture books and, of course, articles and papers for many publications.

Biography: Raymond Eagle: *Seton Gordon. The Life & Times of a Highland Gentleman.* Lochar. 1991.

Seton Gordon in his Cairngorms prime

1

Gaick and Spey

The Gordons lived for many years a few miles north of Aviemore, but earlier on Seton had made several visits to Gaick Lodge so his knowledge of the western flanks of the Cairngorms was extensive, both of the ground and, as seen later, the history and lore of Badenoch and Strathspey.

GAICK

The name Newtonmore is a singular one, the 'more' standing not for *mor* (big), but for the English word *moor*. The Gaelic is Baile Ur an t-Sleibh – the *New Town of the Moor*. Here the river Calder, rising in the Monadh Liath hill range, joins the Spey. Midway between Newtonmore and Kingussie is the House of Balachroan, and above the site of Coulinlinn, ancestral home of an old branch of MacPhersons. It was Captain MacPherson of Balachroan who, with four other deer hunters, was killed by an avalanche while asleep in a bothy on a Christmas night in the year 1799, in the Forest of Gaick. A Gaelic poet describes it as Gaig nan Creagan Grumach, *Gaick of the grim rocks*. Call Ghaig – *the Loss of Gaick* – made so great an impression on the district of Badenoch that old people used to count their years by it and say that they were of such and such an age at the time of the Loss of Gaick.

Kingussie is an old name written Kinguscy as early as the beginning of the twelfth century. This place-name is a memorial of the time when the district stood at the head of the great pine forest of Strathspey, of which a remnant is still found at Rothiemurchus, Glenmore, and Abernethy. The Celtic scholar MacBain gives the original form as Cinn Ghiuthsaich, *Head of the Pine Forest*. Across the Spey from Kingussie is Ruthven Castle near the site of Gordon Hall, the residence of the Gordon lords of Badenoch when Ruthven Castle, their former seat, became a barracks. In 1390 Alexander, son of King Robert II, who was so greatly feared that he received the title of Wolf of Badenoch, lived in Ruthven Castle and from that place made the expedition in which he burnt Elgin Cathedral. His eldest son became Earl of Mar and this title, one of the oldest in Scotland, still survives. In the year 1451 the lordship of Badenoch passed to the Earl of Huntly (ancestor of the last Duke of Gordon who died in 1836) and Ruthven Castle became a seat of the Huntly family, although the original building had been largely demolished and had to be re-built. In 1546 Huntly imprisoned Lochiel and MacDonald of Keppoch in Ruthven Castle; these two chiefs were later convicted at Elgin of high treason and executed. The castle was burnt by a force under Viscount Dundee in 1689 and remained a ruin until Ruthven Barracks were built on the same site in 1718. One of the most outstanding pictures by D.Y. Cameron shows Ruthven Castle standing out in bright sunshine against a dark background.

Near Ruthven Castle the Tromie river enters the Spey. Glen Tromie leads south into the hills. In the neighbourhood of Glentromie Lodge the glen is almost covered with birches where redstarts, tree pipits and spotted flycatchers nest. The tress are soon left behind and at Loch an t-Seilich, *Loch of the Willow*, the hillside rises steeply from the loch. It was at the head of this loch that the avalanche swept down on the party of hunters in 1799; avalanches still periodically occur at this spot and, in or around the year 1922 I remember that a great avalanche from a cornice on the hill high above swept into the birch wood above the east shore of the loch, killing a number of hinds which were sheltering there. There are heavy trout in Loch an t-Seilich and near where the river leaves the loch is a pool where salmon are taken in early summer.

At Gaick Lodge, situated above Loch an t-Seilich, Robert and Guy Hargreaves had the stalking for many years. Both were tireless on the hill. Breakfast in September and up to mid-October was at seven o'clock and by eight the stalkers had left the lodge for distant beats. There was a powerful telescope at the lodge and on a Sunday much time was spent spying the hills and corries for stags, the glass so powerful that deer on the slopes of Sron Bhuirich, two miles to the south appeared quite close.

There is a right-of-way through the hills from Gaick to Dalnacardach in Atholl, past Loch Vrodin [Bhrodainn] and Loch an Duin.

I had a curious experience many years ago on the plateau of a hill south of Loch Vrodin. I was photographing a bird and had been sitting quietly beside my camera for some time when I felt slight pressure against my side. Being intent on my photography I dismissed the occurrence from mind. When I had finished with my bird 'sitter' I made a movement to rise to my feet but found that I was unable to move. I looked round and there, sound asleep, I saw a very small red deer calf lying close to my side for warmth. I then recalled that some time before I had seen a hind running over the hilltop but had thought no more of that incident. I now realised that the hind and her small calf must have been together. It may have been the little one's first expedition and he had insufficient strength to quicken his pace and follow his mother. Seeing me, he had done the next best thing and had walked up quietly and laid himself down in my shelter. When I rose to my feet the small calf attempted to follow me and did so for about half a mile when, becoming weary, he lay down in the heather and there I left him, hoping that his mother would find him.

Loch an Duin (on the county march between Inverness-shire and Perthshire) has high rocks overshadowing it and in these a peregrine falcon for many years had her eyrie. It is a wild loch in storms, the wind sweeping through the narrow pass and lifting the waters high into the air in clouds of grey spindrift. Perhaps under those tempestuous conditions the Witch of Badenoch is abroad (she could assume the form of wild cat or raven) or the Leannan Sith, *the Fairy Sweetheart*, who was wont to appear to hunters in Gaick Forest. Unlike the witch, she was young and beautiful but, like most fairies, capricious and jealous.

HOS-51

FESHIE

By returning to Ruthven Castle and following the road along the south side of the River Spey the River Feshie is reached at Feshie Bridge. Glen Feshie has often been in the news during the last quarter of a century and more because of the suggestion – which has so far come to nothing – that a road should be made through the glen from Braemar to Kingussie to link the valleys of the Dee and the Spey. The road would begin at the Linn of Dee and would follow the Dee westward; after Geldie Lodge it would then cross the watershed at a height of 1,834 feet (Geldie Lodge stands at 1,700 feet) and continue down Glen Feshie. The country all the way is well suited for the making of a road but the cost is prohibitive unless the undertaking should be financed by the Government. At one time I felt that the road would largely spoil the beauty of Glen Feshie but the breath of the Second World War seared this lonely glen. Many of the old pines which had stood in their beauty for centuries were felled, lumber camps were established, roads were driven up the hillsides, and the salmon were dynamited in the river.

Glen Feshie has associations with the great animal artist Landseer and the remains of a frescoe of his on the wall of the small ruined chapel in Glen Feshie were to be seen certainly until a few years ago. On the high rocky face above the chapel my friend Mr. J.C. Harrison, the bird artist, had the rare good fortune to see three snowy owls migrating north on one first day of May. A raven which nested in the rocks flew out over the glen, croaking nervously, and my friend just had time to observe the three great white birds fly over in a stately manner. He made a sketch of the birds, which I have as a record of that unusual scene. The same artist one day when near the top of the Feshie found a clean-run salmon lying on the bank of the river. There was a bite out of the shoulder of the fish and the otters which had their den near the pool, being fastidious feeders, had left the salmon after eating the most tasty portion. My friend, being less particular than the otter, took the salmon home and ate it for several days.

HOS-51

SPEY

Between Loch Insh and Kingussie the river Spey habitually floods the low-lying, almost level land through which it flows, and thus gave the district its name Drowned Lands. It was said of old that the water sprite of the Spey was not satisfied unless she claimed one human victim a year. In 1630 it was written 'Oftimes this river in tyme of speat or stormie weather will be alse bigg as if it were a Logh, and also as broad, and overflowes all the low corne lands of the Countrey next to itself'.

Even when the river keeps to its proper course there are pools and lochans in this low land between Kingussie and Loch Insh and during the winter and early spring months whooper swans make their home here before they fly north-west to their nesting grounds in Iceland. On one winter's day I had the rare experience of seeing the three British swans, Bewick's swan, whooper swan and mute swan, swimming together on Loch Insh.

There are pike and char in Loch Insh and good brown trout, sea trout and finnock. Three or four estates and the parish minister have the right of a boat on Loch Insh. I have not heard of a salmon taking a fly on Loch Insh, the fishing is trolling, the lure a Devon minnow. March, April and May are the best salmon months.

During the war Indian troops were encamped beside Loch Insh; one met them on sequestered forest paths galloping furiously on horseback, crouching on their horses and balancing skilfully on the sharp bends, their black beards streaming in the wind. In appearance some of these Indian hillmen were not unlike the old type of Highland deer stalker, their bearing on foot was erect, they were tireless in walking, their keen eyes flashed. On one occasion, when a troop of Indian horsemen rounding a sharp bend in the forest path almost swept me from it, I wondered to myself what the old people of the district would have said had they been suddenly confronted by what they would have imagined to be apparitions. The Indians went through a long period of training on upper Strathspey and were liked by the natives – and no doubt they felt at home in hill country.

The Spey floaters were a hardy race of men who floated the pines felled in Glenmore and Rothiemurchus down the Spey to the distant Moray Firth. The felled timber was dragged by ponies to the banks of the main streams flowing through the forests and, when all was ready, the sluice gates on Loch Morlich or Loch Eanaich were opened, the logs were thrown into the flood waters and were guided on their course by men of the district armed each with a long pole having a sharp hook at the thin end. When the logs reached the Spey their course was arrested and they were now in the charge of the Spey floaters who fashioned them into rafts equipped with oars. The floaters manoeuvered these unwieldy floats through the rapids of Spey and over its broad, quiet pools until they had reached Arndilly near Craigellachie where a sunken rock in mid-channel usually necessitated local help, given by families of the district. A Hull merchant, William Osbourne, in the year 1785 purchased from the Duke of Gordon the forest of Glenmore. In the space of 22 years he felled the forests and with the timber built at the mouth of the river Spey a fleet of 47 ships. The largest of these was 1,050 tons and she was from the first in the service of the East India Company. The forest was felled at a cost of only £70,000 [see also Chapter 13 'Folklore of Spey and Dee'].

The Spey as it flows through Aviemore and Kinchurdy is still slow for a Highland river although faster than on its sluggish course through the Drowned Lands above Loch Insh. Five miles below Aviemore it flows through Boat of Garten where a bridge spans it. The name Boat of Garten commemorates the era when there were no bridges and when crossing the river was made by boats. Besides Boat of Garten the place-names Blackboat, Boat of Cromdale and Boat of Insh all tell of former ferries. The boat of Boat of Garten continued to transport passengers until the year 1899 when the present bridge was built. The Boat of Cromdale was no longer used when, in 1881, a suspension bridge was built over the river. Two years earlier the Boat of Insh had made its last crossing when a bridge was constructed where Spey leaves Loch Insh. In an account of the Spey the following Boats are mentioned, beginning with Boat of Spey at Fochabers: Boat of Budge, Boat of Fiddich, Boat of Aberlour, Boat of Delnapot, Boat of A'an and Boat of Cromdale.

Shaw in his *History of Moray* names the passage boat of Gartenmore, where stood the house of Cumming of Glenchernich, 'as yet called Bigla's house because Bigla, heiress of Glenchernich, married to the Laird of Grant, was the last of the Cummings that enjoyed that land'. Shaw continues: 'A current tradition beareth that at night a salmon net was cast into the pool below the wall of the house, and a small rope tied to the net and brought in at the window had a bell hung at it which rung when a salmon came into and shook the net.' It must have been worthwhile to have been aroused from sleep in the small hours when a clean-run salmon, waiting to be hauled ashore, was the cause of the disturbance.

HOS-51

2

Western Heights

These hills held a special place in Seton Gordon's affections. Several of his particular studies were made on their heights and when he moved home from Dee to Spey they became his nearest part of the Cairngorms. I've included sorties from both sides, something of Sgoran Dubh, the Moine Mhor and, of course, Braeriach, that hill of hills. We read, what will not be for the only time, of him tramping back to the Derry in the dark after a seventeen-hour day for he lingered, captivated, observant, at one with their world as few have ever been.

EARLY SNOW ON SGORAN DUBH

Rising precipitously from lonely Loch Einich and standing some dozen miles south-south-west from Aviemore is the wild and gloomy hill known as Sgoran Dubh, *the Black Rock*. The most westerly of the Cairngorm range of hills, it is at times mist-capped when its higher and more eastern neighbours, Ben MacDhui and Cairngorm, are clear to their tops and even in June sunshine its precipices have a certain grimness. In early summer when snowfields still linger near the summit, the emerald green of the young grasses and blaeberry plants contrast pleasantly with these snows and with the blackness of the rocks and the result is a blending of colours to delight the eye. Then again, in October, when the grasses become brown and the blaeberry plants turn to rich colours, the hill still shows this harmony of tints.

But one autumn winter came far ahead of her time. Even in September snow lay deep on Sgoran Dubh and big drifts were piled up in every sheltered hollow then, before October was many days old, a second, more severe snowstorm swept the hill. For close on a week the temperature continued below freezing point and a strong and bitter wind brought powdery snow. Even the glen was buried for days beneath a mantle of white and thus I found it when, shortly after mid-October, I paid a visit to the hill. After days of snow and storm the morning opened with blue sky and little wind and although mist still lingered on the tops in Rothiemurchus Forest the sun shone bright and warm. The way led up the Bennaidh, with clear rushing waters sparkling in the sunlight until gradually the last of the fine old Scots firs was left behind and an unbroken expanse of hill and moor met the eye. Some three miles from Loch Einich, about 1,400 feet, the first snow was passed and at the lochside, just over 1,600 feet, three inches covered the ground. Thick ice encrusted the pools in the peat bog. A pair of grouse walked up the track in front of me and were so confiding – or perhaps surprised – that they could scarcely be induced to take wing and although the nearest tree was several miles distant, more than one chaffinch was flitting about the bothy which stands a the lochside. [Long gone; this is *c.*1920.]

Crossing the burn where it leaves the loch, I had a fine view of Choire Odhar – that big corrie at the head of Loch Einich. In summer more than one burn falls in a white cascade down this lonely corrie but today these burns were fast imprisoned beneath snow and ice and the corrie an unbroken expanse of white.

To climb Sgoran Dubh from Loch Einich is, even in summer, a difficult business for there are only one or two gullies which are accessible and with a cornice of snow projecting many feet beyond the ridge these were to-day impracticable. A detour was therefore made northwards, where the hillside is less steep and where a gradually rising ridge could be followed all the way to the summit. My way led me past Loch an-t-Seilich, a small loch concealed amidst great boulders in a slight depression, taking its name from the dwarf willow which grows over its peaty waters and under whose shade trout may be seen to rise in the quiet of a summer's evening. To-day these willows had turned their leaves to a rich brown colour which contrasted curiously with the surrounding expanse of white. Not far off there was borne on the north wind the roaring of stags and soon a number of hinds with two or three stags came into view beneath me, crossing the rocky hill face about Loch an-t-Seilich. At a height of about 2,500 feet I came across a well-grown mountain ash in a rock gorge where there was good shelter from every wind except the east. Beside this hardy tree – still bearing its leaves, withered by frost and snow – were great icicles hanging from the rocks, some the thickness of a man's leg.

As I climbed higher grouse were left behind and I entered ptarmigan country. The eagle was evidently hunting the neighbourhood for the ptarmigan were extremely unsettled and anxious. Either singly or in packs they crossed the hill above me, their flight more rapid and powerful that that of a grouse. Flying noiselessly and looking extremely beautiful, with sky and unbroken snow as their background, the birds soared past me, some with never a movement of their wings. They had not yet assumed the complete winter plumage and I had a fine view of a number of them a little later as they fed on the young shoots of heather. I know that certain authorities have been doubtful as to whether ptarmigan will feed on the common ling (*Calluna vulgaris*) but to-day, and not for the first time, I had undisputed proof for I followed the footprints of the birds till they converged at an exposed patch of heather, the tips of which had all been picked cleanly off.

Notwithstanding the stormy and wintry conditions of last June, ptarmigan seemed to be more plentiful than usual this autumn. Near where the ptarmigan had been feeding were the tracks of a hare and a little farther on a fox had passed up the hill. Recently one of the stalkers of the Forest of Gaick came across a fox almost entirely white. He was anxious to have a shot at it but stags were near and a shot coming at that moment would probably have spoiled the stalk.

Reaching the ridge about the 3,000-foot level, I found an average depth of two feet of snow covering the hill. On each rock and stone feathery ice crystals stood out, fern-like in form. Across the glen, Braeriach was mist-capped but on its lower slopes the air was clear and at times a gleam of sun lit up the snowy expanse. Contrasting strongly with the snow-clad landscape, the dark waters of Loch Einich lay almost immediately beneath me, while south-east from the head of the loch Beinn Bhrotain and Monadh Mor in the Forest of Mar stood out clearly. In a wild snow-clad corrie about a mile to the west a number of stags lay in the snow. I was surprised to see them so far up in such Arctic weather but this particular season the deer were very backward in coming into condition and stalking continued late so that the stags undoubtedly took to the high ground for safety.

My thermometer on the summit plateau showed 31°F – one degree of frost – but the air was milder than earlier in the day and the wind backing to the west brought with it driving clouds so that the summit was soon shrouded in mist and all view obscured. I noticed that day for the first time the curious effect mist and a snow-covered hillside have on the ptarmigan's wings as it takes flight. The white wings are invisible and the bird appears to be flying with its wing-stumps alone.

Suddenly, only a few yards from me, there swept across this snowy wilderness a dark-winged form, gigantic in the mist, for a couple of seconds in view then disappeared in the gloom – a golden eagle in his element. I have often wondered if the eagle, for days perhaps above the mist line, is always sure of his bearings, whether he knows exactly on what hillside he is hunting. Not that it would matter, for the eagle's domain is in the high hills, and he is at home equally in storm or sunshine.

The mist as yet did not descend far and in the valley of the Spey the sun shone warmly. Night descended early so that even the snow did not lighten the gloom. In the Forest of Rothiemurcus stag answered stag in the stillness of the evening and away northward shafts of light pierced the sky as the Aurora flickered in the regions about the Pole.

WON-21

BRAERIACH

Braeriach is greatest of the western Cairngorms, in extent as in wildness; it may even be said to be a hill range. There are not many places on Deeside from which Braeriach can be seen but its summit and north-facing corries show up well from Strathspey. These north corries are, from east to west, Coire Beanaidh, Coire Ruadh and Coire an Lochain. Coire an Lochain, as its name *Corrie of the Lochan* implies, holds in its hollow a tarn, arctic in character, almost always frozen until May or June. I have seen ice-floes on it in early July. On Braeriach I once saw the total eclipse of the sun, on June 29, 1927. My wife and I climbed from the lower bothy in Glen Eanaich by way of the north-west slope of Braeriach, skirting the high rocks of Loch Coire an Lochain. The morning was fine and the sky partly clear of cloud and we left Aviemore at 3 a.m. A thrush and reed bunting were already in song and the air was fresh and calm after heavy rain in the night. On the shoulder of Braeriach before the eclipse the air temperature was 38°F. During the eclipse it fell to 33°F. At the onset of the eclipse the sunlight gradually became dim and a chill air blew across the hill. The sun became sickle-shaped and the light, the strong light of midsummer of the high hills, was replaced by twilight. At the moment of totality the sky resembled that of a winter's night beneath a full moon: the margins of the clouds might have been moon-kissed and the heavens were strange and mysterious. As the sun reappeared the light quickly strengthened, life returned to the earth and ptarmigan bestirred themselves. That season was cold and late. At the end of June ptarmigan had not begun to sit.

On Braeriach is a considerable plateau, the most truly Arctic of any in Scotland. From the west top to the main summit is a distance of a mile and a half and the average altitude over this distance is just over 4,000 feet. Character is lent to the plateau by the Wells of Dee, a number of strong ice-cold springs. The young river they give birth to meanders slowly eastward over the plateau, a shallow, slow-flowing and crystal-clear stream, before quickening its pace and falling in a number of cascades (which are often hidden beneath the snow until midsummer) to the depths of the Garbh Choire, 1,000 feet below. If the climber arrives at the Braeriach plateau from the west and follows the Dee until it falls to the corrie beneath, he has then only to ascend a gentle slope to the summit which is marked by a cairn. To give an instance of the weather conditions which may prevail here in spring, when a friend and I crossed Braeriach on April 3, 1925, we searched in vain for the summit cairn although we knew its location and the weather was clear. It was buried beneath the snow-cap. There must have been an average depth of at least 8 feet of snow frozen so hard that one walked on it as upon firm ground, footsteps scarcely making an impression.

The corries on the north slopes of Braeriach are impressive although in grandeur they are inferior to those on the south side of the hill. Here is that magnificent corrie known as the Garbh Choire (Garrachory, *the Rough Corrie,*) forming the abyss separating Braeriach from Cairntoul. Immediately beneath the summit of Braeriach is Coire Bhrochain, which may mean either *Corrie of Gruel*, or *Corrie of Porridge*, a corrie of grandeur, paved with blocks of granite which have fallen from the hill-top in a past age when some upheaval shook the mountain.

I have looked down into Coire Bhrochain at most seasons but the most impressive occasion was when Bob MacBain of Achnahatanich and I stood here on May 29, 1923. May that year had brought one snowstorm after another on a wind that blew day after day from the north and north-east, bringing the breath of Polar lands to the Cairngorms and even to the glens beneath them. We had climbed from Rothiemurchus to discover how the ptarmigan, which that spring were very numerous, had been affected by the unusual conditions. Even the grouse that year had been compelled to lay their eggs on the snow for their nests had been drifted up. On the morning, within a month of the longest day, an average depth of three feet of snow covered the ground from an elevation of 2,300 feet onwards. We found the ptarmigan population in a state of unrest, for the snow had obliterated the nesting territories of the various cocks, and fights and pursuits were frequent. Even when we had entered the cloud cap the glare from the unbroken snow was trying to the eyes; had the day been sunny we should never have been able to reach the hill-top without suffering snow-blindness.

We reached the summit of Braeriach in early afternoon during a brief lifting of the cloud. The scene was remarkable and probably unprecedented in living memory. Beyond the hill-top a new cornice projected into space over the precipice a distance of some 30 feet; level with the plateau and in thick mist the climber might have walked unsuspectingly onto it. Coire Bhrochain was white, even boulders, rocks and stones were hidden. The whole world in our view was white. A snow tunnel hid the river Dee where it flowed eastward through the Garbh Choire; nowhere in its course through the corrie or where it fell from Braeriach were its waters to be seen. Lochan Uaine of Cairntoul was invisible. Indeed, a stranger looking for the first time would have found it hard to believe that a loch was buried there beneath many feet of snow. Across Lairig Ghru Ben MacDhui seemed weighted down by its great snow mantle; since the snow blizzards had come from the north-east there had been an even heavier snowfall on that hill than on the western Cairngorms. Where, here and there, the summit of Braeriach had been drifted bare of snow by the strength of the wind, the rocks were covered with feathery ice-crystals. They grew to windward on the stones, showing delicate and varied patterns. Ptarmigan that year did not hatch their eggs until mid-July.

The most westerly corrie of Braeriach is named on the Ordnance Survey maps An Garbh Choire Mor, *the Great Rough Corrie*. It is a high, cold corrie, scarcely touched by the sun even at mid-summer, and here lies one of the few so-called perpetual snow-beds in the Highlands. The question [which is answered in Chapter 8 'Eternal Snows' of this book] is "Are there perpetual snow-fields on any hill in Great Britain?"

I must mention the curious tradition of the naming of Coire Bhrochain as told to me forty years ago by old Donald Fraser, deer stalker at the Derry. Donald said that long ago certain cattle, perhaps from the summer shielings in Glen Eanaich, perhaps beasts which had strayed from the drovers on their way to the Falkirk tryst, had fallen over the precipice from the hilltop to the depths of the corrie beneath and by their impact with the rocks had been crushed into gruel or porridge. For many years I looked upon his derivation of the place-name as interesting but fanciful until one summer morning in or about the year 1927 when a companion and I were in the corrie searching for the nest of the elusive snow bunting. We then saw, lying on rough, stony ground, what appeared to be parts of the skeletons of two deer. Being familiar with the tradition my companion sent one of the jaw-bones to an expert for identification. The reply came that it was the jawbone of an ox thus corroborating in a remarkable manner the legend of the name of the corrie. An additional point of interest was that it would have been impossible for cattle to have walked to the place where the bones were lying and the beasts must have fallen over the precipice where their bones, for half the year, are protected from weathering by a covering of snow.

HOS-51

FROM THE DERRY TO BRAERIACH

It was a quarter to five on a cloudless morning in late July. As I stood at my bedroom window in the Castle of Invercauld on the River Dee near Braemar I saw the swifts which nest in the tower fly out into the cold, almost frosty air and climb towards the Lion's Face and its rocks, already a dull gold in the warmth of the rising sun. A quick breakfast and we were off in my friend's Land-Rover on the fifteen-mile drive to The Derry. Braemar village, a hive of activity at this summer season, was still asleep; on Beinn a' Bhuird, the sun shone on the great snowfield known as *The Laird of Invercauld's Table-cloth*. In Glen Lui there were red deer and, when we arrived at Lui Beag, the only cottage in this lovely glen, we found the energetic deerstalker Bob Scott already preparing his porridge to fortify himself for a long day on the river.

We set out for the Lairig Ghru. Monadh Mor on the west horizon held an extensive snow-wreath in its east corrie and there were also pockets of snow on remote Beinn Bhrodain. Close to us, on the heathery slope of Carn Crom, the historic Scots fir, known as *The Tree of Gold*, cast its long shadow across the hill slope. This tree must be centuries old, for native Scots firs, survivors of the ancient Caledonian Forest, grow slowly. I have known this tree for almost seventy years yet I see no change in its height or foliage although some of its neighbours have died and stand naked, white as snow. In olden times cattle raiders from Lochaber, on their way to despoil the rich cattle-rearing lands of the east, are said to have sheltered near here and the place-name, Preas nam Meirleach, survives, *The Robbers' Thicket*. The old hill track to the west on which we walked crosses the *Mam* or Low Shoulder of Carn a' Mhaim and near four miles from Derry Lodge the walker arrives in sight of the highest reaches of Glen Dee and sees great hills rise before him. The Devil's Point and Cairn Toul tower from the west bank of the river and Ben MacDhui from the east. The long ridge of Braeriach forms the north-west horizon. The track descends 200 feet to the River Dee where a footbridge now spans the river and a path leads to the Corrour Bothy. This strong bothan or bothy, built a hundred years ago as a deer watcher's dwelling, is perhaps the only bothy remaining on the Cairngorms; it has been repaired by the Cairngorm Club and is now popular with mountaineers. Strangely enough, it was empty when we looked in, although a pair of black-headed gulls, encouraged no doubt by frequent scraps of food, were hopefully waiting.

This bothy has pleasant memories for me. I recall summers here before the First World War. About 1910 John McIntosh, known as The Piper, was deer watcher, a strong upright man of distinguished appearance – and an excellent piper. In those days Corrour had a box bed. The comfortable mattress for this was laid on the floor for the guest who slept in the warmth of a fire of bog fir and peat. There were few climbers on the hills in those days and when I tuned my pipes outside the bothy door the red deer used to approach and listen; they were obviously excited by the stirring notes.

Our destination was far beyond Corrour so we left it and its warden gulls and climbed the steep slope of Coire Odhar (Corrour its anglicised form). We walked beside a clear burn where the starry saxifrage was in flower and at 3,000 feet above sea level arrived at the small plateau of the Devil's Point where a few late flowers of Alpine azalea opened pink, china-like petals. The sun was warm as we climbed a more gradual grassy slope where winter snowfields still lingered, then granite screes to near the summit of Cairntoul (4,241 feet). We lunched at an ice-cold spring, Clais an t-Sabhail, *the Hollow of the Barn*. I spent many days and nights here before the first war watching a cock snow-bunting, one with an exceptionally loud and beautiful song. The rock which was his main singing post is still there but it is many a year since the snow-bunting nested.

After lunch we toiled across granite screes to look into the deep chasm of Garbh Choire Mor and its snowbed which has melted only twice in the last sixty years. We noticed a pair of ptarmigan dozing in the sun near us. We climbed to the west top of Braeriach and stood at a height of 4,100 feet, at the margin of a broad plateau. This gives a unique view of the Scottish Highlands, near and far. We saw the distant hill of Morven in Caithness on the northern horizon, Ben Nevis and Ben Alder far westward and even Ben Dorain and the hills of the Blackmount Forest in Argyll.

On the plateau where we stood are the Wells of Dee (4,000 feet above the distant North Sea). Never have the waters of the Wells been more appreciated, and enjoyed the more drunk from the ancient silver Highland cup carried by my friend.

Here, almost a thousand feet above the heather line, one is on the roof of the Scottish Highlands and the vegetation may be compared to the tundra of the Arctic. For a short season it is also a natural rock-garden of great beauty where many acres of the delightful cushion pink *(Silene acaulis)* flower. In 1960 my wife and I were here on June 20 when the whole plateau was rose-tinted and towards sunset the sight was one that could never be forgotten. On the present expedition, five weeks later in time, I expected to find the plants in seed but to my surprise few were even in flower and it could be seen that the snow-cover had only recently melted. The season of summer at this elevation varies greatly; indeed, on a visit as long ago as 1907 I found the young Dee entirely invisible beneath the drifted snow of a July blizzard.

Later that afternoon we crossed the plateau near a white quartz memorial stone and looked down onto Loch Eanaich, home of the red-bellied char, above which rose the dark, precipitous slopes of Sgoran Dubh. Beyond the old fir forest of Rothiemurchus flowed the River Spey, a silver ribbon in the westering sun. In the days of steam the whistle of a train at Aviemore station, ten miles distant, could be heard on Braeriach plateau.

It was evening when we set out on our long return walk to The Derry. Our way took us across the deep snowfield near the head of Horseman's Corrie, a corrie which received its name from an enthusiastic tenant of Glen Feshie deer forest many years ago. Descending an easy slope we passed close to Loch nan Stuirteag, *loch of the black-headed gulls*, at almost 3,000 feet. Sandpipers sing and nest here but no black-headed gulls have nested in my time. In recent years, however, a colony of common gulls have nested on its small island and this evening we saw young gulls swimming on the calm water. We now descended into deep dark Glen Giusachan, disturbing a hen ptarmigan brooding closely on a late hatch of seven nestlings. She slipped away silently and they remained almost motionless, a fluffy, contented family.

In Glen Giusachan we were on the traditional hunting ground of the Feinne or Fingalians. These Celtic heroes, who lived before the birth of Christ, are still commemorated in Highland place-names. The name of a deep corrie above the glen is Corie Cath nam Fionn, *Corrie of the Battle of the Fingalians*. Near it rises Beinn Bhrotain and this hill, like Loch Bhrodainn in Gaick Forest, may have associations with the jet-black demon hound named Brodain who was owned by a mythical hunter, perhaps one of the heroic band. Glen Giusachan is a deceptively long glen, especially after a walk of many hours; as we traversed it the shadows were slowly lengthening and the great snowfield on Monadh Mor, which we had seen in bright sunshine early that morning was now in blue shadow.

During the hours we had spent on the high hills the River Dee had risen because of the melting snowfields. We heard the river music as we passed a gigantic boulder precariously deposited by a glacier thousands of years ago on a heathery knoll and at nine o'clock in the evening reached the Dee. The sun, low in the north-west sky, still shone as we searched for a crossing place, for we had reached the river far below the foot-bridge we had used in the morning. The agitated flutings of a bird mingled with the roar of a formidable rushing stream. At last we were across but had to climb 200 feet to reach the path on the shoulder on Carn a' Mhaim, passing on our climb Clais a' Mhadadh, *Hollow of the Wolf*, the lair of one of the last wolves in the Highlands of Scotland. There was still sufficient daylight to follow this path when, an hour before midnight, we saw ahead of us the light in Bob Scott's cottage which we had left seventeen hours before. There was little time for a talk and the Land-Rover was soon carrying us over the rough road to the Linn of Dee. After we had crossed the Linn the road was good but it was half and hour after midnight, as afterglow was merging with sunrise, before we saw the welcoming lights of the Castle of Invercauld.

HS-71

HIGH CAMP AND SUNRISE

Lying a little to the north-west of Cairn Toul and reaching to just under 4,000 feet is the wild and storm-scarred point know in the Gaelic as Sgor an Lochain Uaine, the *Cliff of the Small Green Tarn*.

Eastwards, the ground dips sheer to the Garbh Choire; westwards the land flows away gradually and two hill burns have their birth in the hollows known as Clais an t' Sabhaill and Clais Luineag respectively. This is a wild and barren peak, home to no bird or beast, and few plants – on such exposed rock – are able to find a foothold. At times an eagle, sailing across from Mar or Rothiemurchus, may alight for awhile on its stony summit, or a ptarmigan may shelter behind the rocks on its leeward face should the wind blow strong and cold from the Garbh Choire but it is still a place altogether desolate and given over to the storms and to the hurrying mists.

But when fine June weather comes to the hills and when the sun shines full on ridge and corrie the grim sternness of this weather-beaten point is softened some-what and amongst its granite rocks plants of *Silene acaulis* burst into life and carpet the ground with a profusion of beautiful flowers of crimson or pink while, in the crannies, parsley ferns gradually uncurl their fronds of softest green.

It was early one afternoon of June that two of us left the shores of Loch Einich, that fine hill loch lying beneath the dark rocks and green corries of Sgoran Dubh, and made our way over Coire Dhondail to the wide expanse of high and compara-tively level ground stretching away to the west of Braeriach, known as Moine Mhor, *the Great Moss*. In the corrie much snow still remained where it had been drifted in by a winter's gale from the south-east, and near the ridge a large snowfield hid the track by its steepest and most rocky point. A cock ptarmigan rose ahead of us at an elevation of more than 2,000 feet, an unusually low level, and no doubt he had a sitting mate near.

Great fields of snow still lingered in the Coire Odhar and fringed the corries of Sgoran Dubh: Coire Mheadhon, Coire na Cailliche and Coire nan Each, the brilliant whiteness of their snowbeds contrasting strikingly with the fresh green grass and blaeberry plants growing just beneath. Sailing along the ridges of Braeriach in the teeth of a northerly breeze a golden eagle passed us by, and on the hillside were the feathers of some luckless ptarmigan he had captured. The track reached the plateau of the Moine Mhor at about the 3,000-foot level, and from here a magnificent view lay westward: Ben Lawers, Schiehallion, Ben Alder, Ben Eibhinn, all stood out, their east-facing corries marked with the winter snow.

At our feet lay Loch nan Cnapan, with ice and snow still covering its western shore and perhaps a couple of miles east of it, Loch nan Stuirteag on the march between Mar and Glenfeshie. In Horseman's Corrie the usual extensive snowfield remained and from it flowed a large and swift-flowing burn of beautifully clear water.

Clais Luineag, on its western side, was almost entirely beneath snow and here, beside the source of the burn – which for the first mile of its course was flowing beneath a continuous snow bridge – we pitched our tent at a height of about 3,6000 feet. Towards sunset the wind died away and the stillness was intense. No croak of ptarmigan was to be heard (the snows had driven them lower for nesting) and no song of the snow bunting was carried down to us from the scree above. At 1:30 a.m. we left the tent, making for Sgor an Lochain Uaine, just above us. Though by Greenwich time the hour was but half an hour after midnight, the sky in the north-east was already bright while low down on the western horizon the bright warm light of Jupiter contended with the dawn. Gradually the light strengthened but it was not until seventeen minutes past three that the sun, rising from behind the high ground midway between Cairngorm and Ben MacDhui, transformed the great snow cornice fringing Sgor an Lochain Uaine, bathing it in a pale rose light.

From the time the sun first appeared until his red ball was fully above the horizon exactly five minutes elapsed, and during this time his rays had reached Monadh Mor with its great snowfields and Beinn Bhrotain with its deep corrie facing towards the valley of the Dee. For perhaps half an hour before the sun actually appeared the horizon north-east burned brightly and one single ray shot high into the sky. The waning moon had by now risen above the scree on the western slopes of Cairn Toul and paled in the fast increasing light. On the western horizon lay a bank of dark grey haze, above that a wide band of a greenish tinge merging into a dull pink which reached almost to the zenith. The eternal snows of the Garbh Choire appeared fine, flooded by the rays of the rising sun. Right beneath us lay dark Lochan Uaine, newly freed from its icy covering and so still were its waters that it was hard to distinguish them from the surrounding corrie, and in them reflected images of the many snowfields. Across the wide and rock-strewn Garbh Choire one saw the infant Dee showing for a few hundred yards down the precipitous face of Braeriach before abruptly plunging beneath the snows.

Shortly after sunrise a tiny wisp of thin grey mist commenced to form way down in Glen Geusachan beneath us. Increasing steadily in size, the small cloud, as it rose, caught the rays of sun with fine effect. Gradually filling Glen Geusachan, the cloud overflowed west through the dip in the hills where lies Loch nan Stuirteag, wafted by the lightest of easterly breezes which had sprung up. At the same time a like cloud was forming in the Garbh Choire and away towards the south and south-west similar clouds were lying in the valleys, especially towards the Forest of Gaick. Although the air was apparently mild, a keen frost was binding the ground so that the sphagnum mosses were crisp under foot and a layer of black ice formed on the water issuing from each snowfield, the snow itself hard as iron.

For some time past a cock ptarmigan had been croaking from the boulders of Clais an t' Sabhaill, evidently his mate was brooding somewhere near and the presence of intruders was affording him no little anxiety.

The sun was well above the horizon as we reached the plateau of Braeriach and the hill looked very fine in the clear morning air, the young grasses contrasting strongly with the granite-strewn plateau on which snowfields still lingered. On the plateau an old hind was grazing on the tender grasses. She was remarkably tame, allowing us to approach to within a few yards and then walking on ahead of us with evident annoyance at being so unwarrantably disturbed. But after about fifteen minutes she suddenly got a whiff of our wind and galloped instantly across the shoulder of the hill and beyond our sight.

By nine o'clock, from the precipices of Braeriach, the Garbh Choire presented a wonderful sight. The whole of the corrie and the Lairig were filled with a soft billowy mist, on which the sun shone with almost dazzling brilliance. From this sea the upper reaches of Ben MacDhui emerged and the top of Cairn Toul. Gradually, imperceptibly, despite the power of the sun, the mists rose higher and, as we watched, all ground below the 4,000-foot level was enveloped, though above us the sky was still an unclouded blue. Lawers and Schiehallion for a time kept their summits free but gradually were forced to yield to the advancing vapours. Across the intervening miles Ben Nevis towered, its height seeming enormous, rising from the clouds that lay on hill and glen behind us.

At length, shortly after ten, the mists, in their unrelenting upward course, appeared on the plateau of Braeriach. At first only halting wisps venture thus far, and the sun dispelled them easily, but ever denser, they pressed forward, more quickly too, so that the sun battled in vain again the invading force. Soon the plateau was shrouded in gloom and clammy vapours through which came from time to time the croaking of an unseen ptarmigan and the murmur of the rushing Dee in the Garbh Choire far beneath.

WON-21

AN LOCHAN UAINE

Buried in the very heart of the high hills so no eye can see it from a distance is the loch known in the language of the mountains as An Lochan Uaine, *the Green Loch*. The lochan has many brothers and sisters of the same name but in its own case the designation would appear to be misapplied. Lying in a crater-shaped corrie facing full to the bitter north winds, the lochan is of so great a depth that the bottom cannot be made out, even on a day of strongest sunshine and thus it would seem that the water should be known at An Dubh Lochan, *the Black Loch*.

Winter comes early to the lochan. In the low country the air is yet soft and mild when the first thin sheet of black ice makes its way slowly, quietly out into the dark waters. Many enemies are against this young ice; the springs which feed the loch still retain their summer heat and fierce gusts of wind time and again restore the lochan freedom but, sooner or later, the waters are imprisoned and the lochan sleeps under ice and snow till the coming of another spring. The heart of the deep corrie which cherishes the lochan is over three thousand feet above the level of the distant sea.

The eagle on warm, sunny days perches for hours on end on the hilltop above the loch, enjoying to the full the light and warmth, in winter his form is dark against the snowy wastes and I have seen him speeding up the great glen against a blizzard of powdery snow so dense that it was almost impossible for me to look into the storm.

One summer's day a couple of eagles were hunting above the lochan. On every side ptarmigan swept across the hill in wild flight, anxious at all costs to escape their dreaded enemies. One of the fugitives was struck down by the leading eagle and, as it fell, his mate following, seized the small body and bore it off in her talons, perhaps to a ledge where a hungry eaglet waited.

On sunny days of June and July the wild and beautiful song of the snow bunting is carried down to the loch from the rocky scree above. During this season there is no night on the high hills and this mountain songster may be heard in the intense stillness of the day-break when midnight is but an hour past.

Deer rarely find their way to the lochan, food is scarce on the granite-strewn slopes and the going is steep, even for a stag. Peace is in the glen for this part of the forest is a sanctuary and no rifle breaks the stillness of the corrie or the great glen at any time. During the dark nights of October, maybe, when a southerly wind brings rain and mist low on the hills, the roaring of the stags in the glen below is wafted gently up to the lochan or as the grip of the frost is loosened in the spring and the snow becomes soft, an avalanche thunders from the cornice fringing the ridge above and piles up its debris on the ice-bound waters. The roaring of such an avalanche strikes on the ear like the muttering of distant thunder as the great blocks of snow and ice rush with ever-increasing speed and enormous bounds to Lochan Uaine.

Even during the long days of June it is late before the sun strikes on the dark waters of the lochan for, southward, the ground reaches an elevation of 4,000 feet; for months on end in winter the loch is in deep shadow.

The white mists hang low on the lochan for days together. Sweeping straight across from the distant Atlantic, the winds from the west often carry with them soft fleecy clouds which at first rest lightly on the hill-tops and gradually, imperceptibly, slip down to the surface of the loch. I have often watched from the ridge above the playing of the winds on the waters of the lochan. No air current, except perhaps, from a due northerly point, strikes full on the loch. Often when a westerly wind approaching gale force was sweeping the mountain, I could see the eddying currents meeting on Lochan Uaine and ruffling its waters from every point of the compass, white-tipped wavelet hurried now in one direction, now in another, before the fitful gusts.

On quiet summer days when the lochan lay unruffled by the faintest breeze the veteran watcher of that part of the forest was wont, from the ridge above, to scan the waters of the lochan for the ripple of rising trout but no widening circle of wavelets rewarded his watching. The infant burn which drains the loch descends in a series of cascades to the great glen beneath so that no trout, however active, could force its way up. And then, one hot July day, it occurred to two fishermen that the loch might with advantage be peopled. With no difficulty they succeeded in luring fourteen trout from the big burn and placed them in a large biscuit tin. Then came the diffi-cult part of the undertaking – transporting the future population up the precipitous hillside. The heat was intense, and the water in the tin had to be renewed frequently for the fish rapidly exhausted the limited supply of oxygen and lay gasping on their sides until a new draught was gained and the trout, one by one, were liberated and sent forward into an unknown world.

I have often wondered what was the fate of these trout. Food they must have secured for, during the summer, myriads of small insects play above the surface of the lochan and the depths contain snails and other delicacies. The lochan, too, is of too great a depth for the ice to penetrate far beneath the surface. One can only hope that the explorers are by now firmly established and that the waters of the lochan, lonely from time immemorial, have at last been given small people to cherish in their gloomy recesses.

LHG-20

Jack Harrison, the bird artist, and I were (June 1948) sheltering from a heavy rain squall on the screes near Lochan Uaine watching ptarmigan. A mother and her young, the chicks little more than a fortnight old, rose and flew, or attempted to fly, across an arm of the loch. Young ptarmigan are strong on the wing at a very early stage (they are more precocious than young grouse) but a squall struck the brood and some of them fell into the water at a considerable distance from land. Far from being dismayed, the young ptarmigan swam fast and confidently shoreward, looking like young duck. They reached the shore in a very short time, scrambled over the rocks, and disappeared, as if swimming was an every-day affair.

HOS-51

3

The Bird of Birds

Golden eagles gave Seton Gordon his first (and what would prove a lifelong) special study of a species and he wrote many articles and chapters of books about the 'king of birds', illustrated by his magnificent photographs. Nothing like them had been seen before. He also collected information widely and several of these eagle observations are given. He and his first wife Audrey spent 167 hours observing one Speyside eyrie in 1926 and, with his second wife, Betty, there was an eight-season study of a Skye eyrie.

THE YEARS OF AN EAGLE

When I hear of some old castle lived in for a thousand years by the same family I sometimes wonder whether a pair of golden eagles might not claim that their ancestors in a direct line had nested in the same site for an equal number of years. Birds, fortunately or unfortunately, keep no family records, are the owners of no family tree, so we shall never be able to solve this mystery.

The golden eagle is perhaps longest-lived among birds. There is the record of a golden eagle that was shot in France; engraved on a gold collar round its neck was its name (it had evidently been used in falconry), its native country, and date 95 years earlier. Most of the Gaelic place names in the Highlands are very old. On maps of the Scottish hills and glens will be found a number of place-names Creag na h-Iolaire, *the Eagle's Rock*. This Celtic name persists in districts where, at the present day, Gaelic is no longer a living language. In certain of these 'eagle's rocks' the golden eagle still has its eyrie. There are others where the birds are no longer to be found but one such rock, which I never thought would see an eagle again, has in recent years been once more occupied by a pair of these grand birds, perhaps the descendants of the pair which gave their name to the rock.

As a boy I used, forty years ago (*c*.1903), to watch a pair of golden eagles at their eyrie on a certain rock. Now, in the summer of 1943, they are still nesting on the rock. Another eyrie, which to my knowledge has been tenanted regularly during the past thirty-seven years, in a native Scots pine growing in a high glen almost 2000 feet above the sea. When first I knew that eyrie it was three or four feet deep and was built three quarters of the way up the tree. When I visited it in the early summer of 1943, it reached the treetop and the latest nest was actually the highest part of the tree. The whole structure had the appearance of a number of wicker baskets piled one on top of the other and was approximately fifteen feet high. The pine is an old one (perhaps 300 years) and each spring it must bear an increased weight, which may now exceed a ton.

Golden eagles' eyries in trees are sometimes blown down by winter gales and the wonder is that this does not happen more frequently for the tree chosen is almost always an outlying one on an exposed hillside where no neighbouring trees impede the eagle in her take off from the nest. One pair of eagles nested in a birch tree. I visited their glen for the first time for twenty-nine years and the birch, gnarled and solitary, was still there but the eyrie had fallen.

HY-44

EYRIE BUILDING

Only recently have I had the good fortune to see an eagle actually choose a new nesting site. I watched her and her mate carry in the first heather and, as we humans might put it, lay the foundation stone of the new home. Golden eagles are kingly and conservative birds. Most pairs own two eyries, some three or even more. The foundations of these eyries last and there is thus no need to construct a complete new eyrie in the Arctic weather that goes by the name of Spring in the Highlands. True, March may come in like the proverbial lamb and the sun was warm that day as I began my watch near Creag na h-Iolaire, *the Eagle's Rock*.

That morning the female eagle, gliding low above the grassy rabbit-haunted slopes below the cliff, had climbed on the light east wind and disappeared in the distance. She returned and alighted for thirty seconds on an eyrie she had built some years before. I imagined she had chosen that eyrie for her rearing of a family but I was wrong. She rose and disappeared over the cliff-top then almost at once reappeared, flying fast and straight towards the cliff face. Skilfully she avoided the crash-landing that seemed imminent and alighted on a ledge, placing in position the heather plant she was carrying. She rose, circled several times, then landed on the grassy slope a few feet below the rock. Grasping a tussock of rough grass in one foot she dragged it from its root-hold, took wing, but dropped it before she reached the ledge. She was evidently undecided and stood there awhile as if thinking out a problem. After a short flight, she returned to the heathery ledge and began her task of nest-making. The new eyrie had as yet no shape; she settled down in a brooding position and began to scrape, turning on her breast as she did so. Slowly she hollowed out a nesting cup, all the time lying so flat on the nest that I could only just see her. Now and again, still prostrate, she scraped out the debris with her feet. It was hard work. She stood up, rested for a few seconds then flew fast towards a neighbouring hill.

Her mate appeared and, tightly closing his wings, dropped several hundred feet in a display dive. Straightening out, he followed his mate at his best speed. The dark form of an eagle against the blue of a sunlit sky is a memorable picture, especially so on this occasion with a young moon, white and cold in full daylight, as a background.

Three days earlier I had seen the male eagle make a spectacular approach to the rock. A strong and stormy south wind was blowing and for a moment I saw a dark object falling headlong. The cliff hid him until he was almost overhead and I saw him flying so fast that it seemed he must overshoot the nesting site. An exciting display of skilled diving followed: he suddenly closed his wings and fell headlong. Because he had been moving horizontally the dive was slanting rather than vertical – and the more breath-taking because of this.

Almost a year before I saw the same eagle give an impressive flying display for the benefit of his mate as she stood near the top of the cliff. In quick succession he brilliantly accomplished one high aerial dive after another, after each dive returning to his original height with quick, eager thrusts of his powerful wings. Still rising, he would suddenly close his wings tightly, his impetus causing him to rise still further in the unusual position. His impetus almost exhausted he would put his head down and skilfully use his tail to bring him into a diving position. At first he fell slowly then faster and faster until, near the ground, he levelled off, using his travelling speed to aid the next upward flight.

The golden eagle also performs stunt flying and diving during the season of mating. On that very afternoon she visited her unfinished eyrie and then delighted me with a long spell of climbing and diving with great *joie de vivre*. Once, half-way through her dive, she dropped into a tightly packed flock of starlings. At that distance the starlings seemed no larger than gnats as they scattered in alarm. The eagle shot through them as though they did not exist. (Birds of prey do not eat starlings unless really hungry; their flesh is not tasty.)

HS-71

MATING JOYS

The March blizzard had deeply covered the hills and the eagles' rock rose grim and lonely beneath a sombre sky. High on this snowy rock were the two eyries which the eagles have used in alternate seasons during the past twenty years. Now, when the eagles should have been busy at their house repairs, the eyries were buried and unrecognisable beneath the snow which lay on each ledge of that high cliff.

I have watched the home life of these eagles for the twenty seasons they have nested here and have come to know how near the observer can approach and sit without alarming the birds. It was cold on the sunless, snowy slope and I was about to end my watch for there had been no sign of the eagles nor the pair of ravens which rather unwillingly share the eagles' territory. The eagle-watcher often experiences an unexpected thrill at the moment he is preparing to leave and it was fortunate for me that I was reluctant to start for home.

The two golden eagles appeared, coming suddenly into my view from the far side of the cliff. The male was leading. He is smaller than his mate but I have also come to recognize him by his poise and by his buoyant and almost delicate soaring. He is, besides, unusually attentive and when the eggs were near hatching I have watched him almost push his mate off the eyrie in order to take his share in incubating the eggs during this critical period. Now, within a week of when the eggs should be laid, the two eagles seemed to be taking life easily, with no thought of rearing a family.

Pesticides used in sheep dip are thought to be changing the golden eagle's pattern of life and, indeed, so far as I could tell, this pair of eagles reared no young during the season of 1964. Was the coming season to be a barren one also? The female eagle rose buoyantly for she felt the uprising current beneath a passing snow cloud. From a height of several hundred feet she glided gracefully down and alighted on a rock spur above the precipice. In less than a minute her mate alighted close to her. They stood there in proud and majestic beauty – the King and Queen of Birds!

Her mate walked up to her, jumped lightly on to her back and mating took place. His six-foot wings were outspread and half-raised. This mating lasted perhaps a couple of minutes when the male eagle sprang lightly into the air and disappeared from view. Then came a most impressive joy flight by his mate, rising to a great height on an air current she closed her wings and pressed them tightly against her flanks, going into an almost vertical dive. When near the ledge where one of the eyries is situated she suddenly straightened out, sailed to her former height and again performed that exciting headlong descent.

On this March afternoon the female, after her aerobatics, had scarcely alighted on her rocky perch when a pair of ravens, her neighbours on the same heathery cliff, passed over at a great height. Travelling fast, one of the ravens with a sudden movement turned on its back and for a second flew upside-down in unique raven fashion.

The previous afternoon I had watched the eagles hunting. A fresh north-easter was blowing across the cliff and the eagles were hunting it carefully for their main food, the rabbit. They would glide at great speed downwind across the snowy slope then slowly move up against the wind, dark object casting still darker shadows on the white, snow-filled gullies. Small avalanches were falling from a cornice along the hill top and the eagles dropped suddenly to the falling fragments of snow and carefully inspected them. Near sunset one of the eagles during the patrol up-wind made a sudden, rapid slant to lower ground. His keen eye had detected a rabbit which he killed instantly and carefully plucked the fur from the carcass before enjoying his supper. He then lifted the remains and, as he slowly rose in spirals, looked like a miniature airship. Having gained sufficient height he sailed in and alighted on a ledge near the eyrie where he was joined by his mate and perhaps shared his supper with her.

HS-71

ENCOUNTERS

Seton Gordon collected many first-hand accounts of eagle behaviour besides being such a keen observer himself. In the following where Seton Gordon quotes from corre-spondents, the paragraphs are in single quotation marks. Unless otherwise noted they are from Days with the Golden Eagle.

Once, on the plateau of Beinn A'an, I saw the fur and skin of a fox scattered over the ground and I have little doubt that an eagle, coming upon a fox (perhaps a young animal) unawares, had killed it and made a meal there and then. I have received a number of interesting accounts of fights or sparring matches between fox and eagle. Old John Ferguson of Badenoch, a stalker of many years' experience, told me how he approached an eagle's eyrie unobserved and noticed a fox half-way down the rock, attracted by the ptarmigan in the eyrie. Overhead the two parent eagles were soaring. The fox soon saw that he could not reach the larder and evidently did not think the spot a healthy one with the eagles so close; he climbed the rock and trotted off across the moor, holding his brush straight up in the air. Ferguson thinks he did this, as he put it, "better his tail should be attacked than himself."

On another occasion Ferguson was out stalking with a gentleman. They were near the top of a hill when the stalker saw what he thought was the antler of a stag in velvet crossing the skyline. Ferguson was afraid that they had disturbed the deer which were ahead of them and kept very still. But the fancied stag in velvet was only a fox. An eagle was soaring close above him and this fox also was holding his brush straight in the air since the eagle was too near for his liking. The supposed antler in velvet was the fox's brush!

One day, when Ferguson was visiting his traps in Glen Feshie, he came to where he had set a trap on either side of a bait and found a golden eagle in one trap and a fox in the other. He tells me the best method of trapping a fox is by setting two traps; if a fox is at all suspicious of a bait he waits to see if something is caught. For example, when he sees a hooded crow struggling in a trap the wily fox thinks to himself, "Now the trap has caught somebody it cannot catch me," so he walks up and eats his fill. Thus the trapper has to match cunning with cunning. On this occasion Ferguson believes the fox must have seen the eagle trapped and chuckling to himself come in on the other side – and was caught too! The eagle was alive but very weak because of its long imprisonment in the trap. Sorry to find an eagle caught, he carried the great bird home and kept it for some time in a shed hoping it would recover. In a few days it became so tame that it would allow the stalker to open its bill and push small pieces of venison down its throat.

• • •

Observers have recorded what can only be described as games played by eagles. The game may be played with a grouse of ptarmigan or some inanimate object. A deer-stalker told me of a remarkable scene he saw. The female eagle appeared carrying a black object with which she rose to a great height. She dropped what she was carrying, allowed it to fall a little way, then dived after it, dropped at great speed considerably beyond it, abruptly checked her fall and, as she rose a little way with the impetus she had gained, caught the object in her foot. She repeated this performance several times. Her mate then appeared and took his part in the game. She dropped the object from a great height but this time did not attempt to overtake it; the male overtook and caught it. The two eagles at last tired of the game and dropped the object, this time for good. The plaything was found to be a hard, dry piece of moss.

GE-55

• • •

'One day in April my father was having a round of the sheep when he heard what he thought were the cries of a child in distress. Crossing a small knoll he saw two golden eagles in deadly embrace. As he approached them he thought the undermost bird caught sight of him but it was held down by its antagonist which was so absorbed in the struggle that it paid no heed to his approach. He caught the top bird by the wings and placed his foot on the under one. Searching his pockets, he found he had nothing to tie the wings with, ultimately doing so with a bandage removed from an injured hand. Meantime the other bird had by degrees pulled free and after several attempts managed to soar away. At a cottar's house a sack was procured and my father carried the monarch of the air home. The capture was kept in an attic room for six weeks, being fed on hares, rabbits, and dead lambs. He rarely touched the food in our presence but we enjoyed viewing operations through the keyhole.'

• • •

Sometimes two male birds engage in desperate battle and a friend writes that he found an eagle dead after a fight and the victor so injured that it scarcely could flutter away. The dead eagle had its gullet torn out. In a lonely deer forest a pair of golden eagles was seen to fall, locked together, from a great height and likely to be dashed to death on the ground. When they had almost reached the earth they separated, checked their descent with their great wings and easily alighted. They faced one another and for a time stood still, necks outstretched and all their feathers raised. An armistice was arranged and both eagles flew away.

ITH-31

• • •

From sixty correspondents, all of whom have lived in the country of the eagle, I have heard of only about a dozen authentic instances of an eagle being seen to take living lambs, yet these men are out on the hills daily and at all times of the year. The evidence collected seems to point to eagles probably taking to lamb killing only when food is scarce and with some eagles it becomes a habit. But they prey on lambs only during the first four weeks of their lives, while the eagles are rearing their own young. As eagles can actually kill deer (up to the age of a year) it follows that if they liked they could kill even a sheep yet the keepers and shepherds agree that they attack only young lambs. Why do they not attack sheep? It cannot be a question of weight; they could feed on the carcase where they killed it as they do on large deer calves which they kill. The conclusion is that sheep and lambs are really an unnatural prey only taken in exceptional circumstances.

• • •

Eagles seem to take pleasure in alarming deer. I have more than once seen them swoop down close to a heard of grazing stags, causing the animals to shift their ground uneasily and one of the very few times I have ever heard a golden eagle call was just after one of these playful stoops when his mate, sailing near, was watching. A head stalker saw a pair of eagles pursuing and swooping at a herd of hinds and calves. Eventually the eagles separated a hind and a calf from the main herd and, buffeting the calf with their wings, drove it over the precipice toward which they had been endeavouring to herd the deer. The calf was killed by the fall and the eagles proceeded to devour it.

• • •

'I had just stalked and shot a stag out of a small mixed lot of stags and hinds and was keeping the herd under observation when an eagle stooped on and struck a calf a terrific blow with her body. As far as I could see the eagle did not attempt to fix her talons or bill in the calf, she simply swooped down at a terrific pace, her wings folded and legs close up to her body. Scarcely had she ascended when another eagle attacked in the same manner, and then a third. All three birds adopted the same method of attack and confined their attentions to the same animal. Being September the calf was pretty well grown and avoided a good many of the blows by wheeling sharply as one of the big birds approached; but attack followed attack so quickly that he very soon got exhausted and then one of the eagles fixed her talons in his withers and, flapping her huge wings savagely, bore the calf to the ground.'

• • •

I have few records of encounters between roe-deer and eagle. In the Forest of Gaick a roebuck was seen being attacked by an eagle. The plucky roe showed no signs of fear but rose on his hind legs and struck out at the surprised eagle with his forelegs until the eagle made off. Another roebuck was attacked in Glen Feshie. The buck was feeding at the edge of a birch wood when an eagle suddenly swooped and struck at the roe, who dodged the blow and bounded for the nearest clump of trees, where he continued to graze unconcernedly.

• • •

Eagles capture strange prey at times. I have seen several squirrels in an eyrie and more than one stoat. A shepherd was on the hill when an eagle rose near him; he found the bird's kill – a ferret. A ferret is a formidable animal for even the eagle to kill; perhaps this one was asleep in the sun and was taken unawares. When disturbed the bird had not begun to feed but had partly skinned the ferret and had torn some of its fur off.

HY-44

• • •

Other eagle prey noted among Seton Gordon's writings are fox cubs, lamb, roe and red deer calf, weasel, water-vole, dog, grouse, blackcock, magpie, hoodie, rook, seagull, heron, pike and salmon (originally caught by an otter).

A friend has told me the remarkable story of how a pair of golden eagles were made to provide a shepherd and his family with the best of good things for several months. The shepherd found an eagles' nest in a low rock so he walked into the eyrie and helped himself to the grouse and blue hares which were lying beside the two eaglets. On returning home and being complimented by his wife, he formed a plan to go each day to the nest and bring back a part of the eagles' prey. The eagles perhaps imagined that their youngsters had unusually healthy appetites but by strenuous hunting kept both families supplied with food. In time the eaglets were feathered and the shepherd grew anxious. He saw the days of his plentiful menu numbered. Accordingly he tethered each eaglet firmly to the nest. When August came the eaglets were still there but a few days before the "Twelfth" they were given their liberty and the shepherd and his wife had to live hard for a time.

ITH-31

4

Lairig Ghru

The Lairig Ghru is regarded as the most impressive, most demanding and perhaps most dangerous of our passes yet has been a pedestrian route through the Cairngorms for centuries and all who explore the range come to know it well. The summit of the pass lies at 833 m (2,733 feet) and the distance from Aviemore to Braemar on 30 miles, which makes some of what follows impressive – as were Seton Gordon's many journeys through the pass or his stopovers at Corrour bothy.

AN OCTOBER CROSSING OF THE LAIRIG

Towards noon one early October the wind shifted west (a good weather sign), the clouds lifted and I set out from Glen Derry in Mar on my journey through the Lairig to Rothiemurchus on Speyside. The wind was soft and mild and as I struck west Beinn Bhrotain and Monadh Mor – the two big hills that guard the Lairig near its southern end – showed darkly through the mist. The Luibeag burn was in spate, its waters having that characteristic appearance of 'snaa bree.' From where the track crosses the burn near the foot of Carn a' Mhaim the south-facing corries of Ben MacDhui presented an almost unbroken surface of snow. But amongst the storm-scarred pines in the glen, winter had not yet obtained the mastery and cranberries, fully ripe, still showed in sheltering places and trout splashed in the shallows of a small burn.

As I rounded the shoulder of Carn a' Mhaim, where the path just touches the 2,000-foot level, a heavy rain squall from Glen Geusachan swept across, blotting out hill and glen but soon passed by so the steep and rocky spur of the Devil's Point stood out, corniced with snow and, lying snugly at its base, the lonely, small Corrour bothy. I do not remember having seen the Dee here running in bigger spate for the sudden thaw on the hills had brought much snowwater from the corries and the rushing of the river carried far in the stillness of the glen.

Cairn Toul was hidden in mist but Ben MacDhui was clear with glimpses of sunlight showing up the great snow wreath lying at the head of Coire nan Taillear, *the Tailor's Corrie*, and the burn, running fast and strong, suddenly emerging half-way down the hillside from beneath the snow. Poised just above the ridge of Ben MacDhui was a small, dark object which, through the glass, was revealed as a peregrine falcon. He hung motionless in the teeth of a strong breeze, hovering like a giant kestrel as he scanned the ground beneath him. After a time, swinging round in a circle, he searched another part of the hillside and here seemed to spy something for he dropped again and again, hovering motionless between whiles until he had reached a point only a few yards above the ground. I do not know whether he secured his quarry, watching him was difficult in the uncertain light.

I have rarely, if ever, seen finer colours of light and shade on the Cairngorms. Between the showers the air was exceptionally clear and the snow-freed corries and slopes were of an extraordinarily deep blue and appeared wonderfully near. Even the snow at times took on a pale blue tone. Inky black clouds spread across the hills from the west and then almost instantly disappeared, to be replaced by a sky of turquoise blue.

I passed the first snow near the Pools of Dee. Even at this height (on the 3,000-foot level) the air was mild for the steep face of Sron na Lairige sheltered the pass from the strong breeze. Snow wreaths lay around the Pools of Dee and in the pools themselves there floated remnants of snow and ice. Some of the hill ferns, protected from the frost by their covering of snow, were still green and the grasses were indeed more green than in the glen below. The leaves of many blaeberry plants lay scattered on the surface of the snow for, unlike the cranberry, the blaeberry is one of the most sensitive of hill plants to a sudden frost. Through the snow a well-marked track indicated where stags had been crossing from Mar to Rothiemurchus in the quest for hinds.

I had reached the summit of the Lairig without encountering a single ptarmigan but on the watershed a cock *tarmachan* rose from the hillside above me and flew at a considerable height and with zig-zagging flight across the pass, alighting carefully on a snowfield. Through the glass I could make out his plumage to be in the transition stage but with the white feathers of the winter dress predominating. I felt confident, by the flight of the bird, that I was not the cause of his alarm and sure enough, on looking round, I spied the hereditary enemy of the ptarmigan – the golden eagle. Sailing leisurely through the Lairig the great bird passed right over the spot where the ptarmigan was crouching – seemingly without noticing him – and making on towards Cairngorm.

A few minutes later a covey of some six or seven ptarmigan came flying wildly from the direction in which the eagle had disappeared. A second time the eagle beat up the pass and I thought I heard him call shrilly once, before he sailed up into the mist-filled corrie and was lost to view.

A last backward glance showed Cairn Toul and the Devil's Point, very dark against the sun-flecked sky, and away to the south'ard the big hill of Beinn a' Ghlo, mist-capped, but with large snowfields on its lower slopes. Northwards the valley of the Spey was in sunshine while, behind it, stood out the broad outline of Ben

Wyvis and, farther away, the conical peak of, I think, Ben Mor Assynt. Wind now rushed through the Lairig from the north, in gusts attaining the force of a gale and at times catching up the waters of the March burn and turning them into spin-drift.

In the calm intervals the roar of the wind in the rocks mingled with the rush of the burn and in the dark, swirling mists and great snow-filled corries, one felt that here indeed was the very heart of the hills.

A couple of miles below the summit of the pass I saw a covey of grouse flying in the same agitated manner as the ptarmigan and in this case also an eagle was the cause of alarm.

And now the woods of Rothiemurchus were showing: big areas of Scots firs interspersed, here and there, with weeping birches with foliage of golden tint, or rowans with their leaves of sombre red. And what a wonderful crop of rowan berries covered the trees, so heavy were the clusters of fruit that the whole tree in some cases drooped.

Many stags were roaring in the early twilight of the October afternoon, one in particular, a fine heavy beast with a good head, threw out his challenge persistently with a deep, strong voice.

Looking backward now, the whole range of the Cairngorms stood out in the fading light. Apparently from the position of the wreaths there had been two distinct driftings of snow: one from the north-west and north, the other from a southerly direction. For one minute the summit plateau, Arctic in appearance, stood out before being quickly shrouded in cloud once more.

Low in the western sky the new moon shone brightly. Darkness came quickly in the forest of pines and with its coming the roaring of the stags increased. A wood-cock rose at my feet, flitting off quietly in the twilight and the murmur of the wind in the firs and the rushing of the hill burn were borne pleasantly to the ear at the close of the day.

WON-21

LAIRIG OBSERVATIONS

In former times there was much crossing of the Lairig by the people of Mar and upper Strath Spey. Young girls of Rothiemurchus used to cross the Lairig in threes and fours to Deeside villages. I believe that an old man who lived in Rothiemurchus was in the habit of taking the long walk merely to have a *ceilidh* or talk with the stalker in Glen Derry, and, talk ended, thought nothing of the sixteen-mile tramp back across the hills.

CHS-25

On a dark, thundery day I was traversing the Cairngorms, the air heather-perfumed on the lower slopes. At the Pools of Dee I reached a favourite haunt of the ptarmigan and first one, then several of these white-winged birds, rose snorting from the grey rocks. The ptarmigan I had expected to see; the small flight of teal which rose from one of the Pools and winged their way fast southward where unexpected. I had never before seen any bird save a dipper on the Pools of Dee. They lie nearly 3,000 feet and there is no vegetation growing in their ice-cold waters. The teal (late August) were probably on migration.

I had walked across from Aviemore to Braemar to assist in the judging of the piping at the Braemar Gathering and as I was expected to do the same thing at the Kingussie Gathering the next day it was necessary for me to return through the Lairig Ghru very early the next morning in order to reach Kingussie in time. It was a perfect morning. I saw the sun rise on Braeriach and Cairn Toul and shortly after its rising reached the Pools of Dee. There, in the faery light of that glowing sun, I wondered for an instant if my eyes were not playing me a trick for I saw what at first glance appeared to be small animals travelling snakelike at tremendous speed along the rock-strewn pass. Then I realised that these were no terrestrial creatures but a flight of swallows, winging their way toward the south a foot or more off the ground. So low did they fly that I could look down on them and admire the lovely dark-blue plumage of their back. Like the teal, there were on migration and had perhaps passed the night somewhere along the valley of the Spey and before sunrise had set off on their journey through the hills.

HY-44

When I crossed the Cairngorms after judging at Braemar and then walked through the hills during the night to judge at Kingussie next day I tried unsuccessfully to persuade some of the competing pipers to accompany me but they preferred to travel by bus and train rather than cross the hills in the dark – a distance of twenty miles. The second occasion on which we did this, my friend and I had so dark a night for our walk that we could scarcely see our hands in front of our faces. The king sent me a letter through his equerry which ran, "When the King heard the rain in the small hours of the morning His Majesty hoped that you were enjoying yourself".

HOS-51

As we passed the Tailors' Stone, *Clach nan Taillear*, grouse were crowing cheerily. Clach nan Taillear is a large flat-topped boulder standing at the base of Carn a' Mhain opposite Coire Odhar. Certain tailors, to the number of three or more, one winter long ago wagered that within twenty-four hours they would dance at the "three dells", – Abernethy, the Dell of Rothiemurchus, and Dalmore near Braemar. They danced at Abernethy and Rothiemurchus but a blizzard of snow overtook them in the Lairig and they died in the shelter of the stone that now bears their name.

There is a Tailor's Stone on Cairngorm too but the story of this stone is a cheerful one. A certain tailor was also a keen stalker. At the season when the Mar stags were in the habit of crossing to Glen More Forest to seek the hinds this tailor, taking his cloth and his gun to the hill, used to sit at his work upon this stone, all the time keeping a sharp look out for any stag that should come within shot.

CHS-25

At Corrour bothy I was surprised to see a small bird fluttering about the room. When it came to rest on the window I identified a golden-crested wren. Evidently the little stranger was migrating south for this locality was totally unfitted for his requirements, close on 2,000 feet and the nearest tree many miles distant. How he came to take up his abode in such strange quarters is a mystery; an isolated bothy would present little or no attraction to a migrant. The goldcrest migrates in enormous flocks and every spring and autumn great numbers are killed by dashing against lighthouses.

COH-12

The ground at the Pools of Dee was deeply covered with snow. I noticed a small dark speck and curiosity led me to the spot. I found a robin redbreast, lifeless on the snow. The poor little fellow must have been overtaken by a blizzard when on migration for, even in summer, no robin is found on the Cairngorms (they have their home in the old forest far beneath those wind-swept slopes). Often in my mind I picture the tragedy of that lonely robin, battling against wind and drift, weakening gradually, then falling exhausted amid the unheeding snows, that immortal spark of indestructible spirit within him swiftly seeking the great unknown.

Birds often succumb to cold and storm when crossing the high Cairngorms. I have at different times found the mummified remains of lapwings and thrushes 4,000 feet above sea-level on the melting of the snows.

ITH-31

JOURNEYING TO CORROUR

In those days a wonderful excursion train left Aberdeen each Wednesday and Saturday at one o'clock in the afternoon, ran to Aviemore, returning the same night, the first-class return fare half a crown! That was in the days of the Great North of Scotland Railway which lost its soul when it was amalgamated with the L.N.E.R. which in its turn has parted with its identity and is now unrecognised among British Railways. That afternoon excursion to Strathspey from Aberdeen was really a remarkable achievement. The first stop was Craigellachie, sixty-eight miles from Aberdeen and was reached in eighty-five minutes – a much slower journey at present. On that occasion we had received permission to ride in the cab of the locomotive and I remember how worried the driver was as we rushed through Kintore thirty-five seconds late! I was on the foot-plate as far as Craigellachie, and Malcolm then took my place as far as Aviemore. Incidentally, he (now Sir Malcolm Barclay Harvey of Dinnet) later wrote the *History of the Great North of Scotland Railway*. After travelling at high speed non-stop to Craigellachie the train was booked to call at most of the stations along the Spey and, leaving the Great North of Scotland Railway at its terminus at Boat-of-Garten, the engine and carriages then travelled the extra distance of five miles to Aviemore by permission of the Highland Railway (which later became part of the L.M.S. system). When at Craigellachie, my friend changed places with me in the cab of the locomotive, I seated myself in the first class compartment he had just left, no doubt depositing soot and grime on its dark-blue cushions.

Having for the sum of half a crown been carried from Aberdeen to Aviemore first class – for which privilege we should now have to pay several pounds and should spend a whole day on the journey – we set out in the late afternoon on our walk through the Cairngorms by way of the Lairig Ghru. The day was fine and there was little or no wind. In the forest of Rothiemurchus the blaeberries and the cowberries were ripening and the sun was drawing the resinous scent from the pines. Darkness had come when we passed near the Pools of Dee and I recall the light of a bright planet reflected in the still waters. Ptarmigan, roused by our passing, croaked sleepily. The Lairig at the watershed is stony and the path in places difficult to follow. A hundred years ago there was a certain amount of trade between Strathspey and Braemar and, as ponies sometimes crossed between the two districts, the path at the stony watershed was kept clear but for more than half a century nothing has been done to it and in darkness it is not easy to follow. It was after midnight when we reached the neighbourhood of Corrour bothy. A small cloud on Cairntoul had flowed into Lairig Ghru and through the cloud we walked, knowing by the land-marks on the track when was the correct moment to strike off to reach and cross the river and climb the short distance to the bothy. So close was the mist, we were able to locate the bothy only by the murmur of the burn that flows down from Corrour (Coire Odhar) close to the small building. We knew the hiding place of the key, thanks to John Macintosh, and we groped our way into the one small room and lit the candle set ready on the table. The peat fire had to be coaxed into life, water fetched from the spring, and the kettle boiled. The bothy in those days was so clean that we slept on a mattress on the floor. The wee room had a homely and hospitable feeling such as no other room I have lived in, either before or since. It was good to hear the grouse crowing outside the bothy when one awakened early in the morning and saw the sunshine on the green ledges of Carn a' Mhaim so that they seemed to glow, intangible, in mystic light. I have a clear memory of opening the bothy door on that particular August morning. The air was still and silent and dew lay thick on grass and heather. The whole air was perfumed by heather blossom, not the strong scent of heather in sunlight but an aroma very delicate and pure such as I never remember having experienced either before or since. The great hills – Cairn Toul, the Devil's Point, Ben MacDhui – seemed near and friendly. All the world was at peace and it was good to share the peace which lay at the heart of nature. I have stayed many times in the Corrour bothy, at all seasons of the year and I have never left it without a feeling of regret, yet that particular morning stands out in my memory.

HOS-51

THE WORST BLIZZARD

Arriving at the bothy we soon had a fire burning from the store of peat and bog fir. It was either the next day or the day after that the most severe blizzard I have ever experienced struck the Cairngorms. There was little that afternoon to tell that the blizzard was near but as we climbed to the corrie above the bothy we became aware that the ptarmigan, of which there was a large stock, were behaving in an unusual manner. The birds were arriving, some flying, others running, from the higher grounds. Later in the day when we returned we found ptarmigan crouching for shelter in our foot-marks in the snow where our feet had broken through the frozen crust.

The blizzard was near when we reached the bothy. Snow was already falling and drifting but it was not until darkness fell and was soon dispelled by the moon that the storm was at its height. In the moonlight the Lairig was almost as light as day. The snow had ceased to fall and overhead stars could be seen but, across the ground and up to a height of six feet and more, snow, white and solid as a blanket, was drifted furiously by the frost-laden gale out of the north. We piled the fire high with fuel yet in that small room a basin of water, placed on the table beside the window, eight feet from the fire, froze. Next morning the storm abated. Everywhere snow lay deep; the river was invisible. Snow had been drifted over it, and when half-melted by the water had frozen as a sheet of ice, which again had been covered by fresh snow.

The weather gradually improved, yet on the morning when our stay at the bothy ended and we were to walk down to Derry Lodge we were uncertain whether to go by the pass or to climb over Ben MacDhui. We decided to go over the hilltop as we had less weight to carry than when we arrived but my pipes in their case were not handy things to transport up a steep icy slope. We climbed by way of the Tailors'

Corrie and when we saw the Tailors' Stone thought that the tailors who perished there might have been the victims of a storm such as we had so recently experienced. Near the top of the corrie the plateau of Ben MacDhui falls away in a steep, scree-strewn slope, in places almost precipitous. The slope is so steep that when the hot weather comes the snow sometimes breaks away as an avalanche; one summer day when I was passing beneath the corrie this actually happened, great blocks of frozen snow hurtling down the hillside with the noise of thunder.

When we stepped out on to the summit plateau we might have been polar explorers completing our journey. We were in a dead-white world where no life stirred. The depth of snow was so great that even stones and boulders were hidden. This made walking easier yet the cold was intense and the frost-laden wind bitter. MacDhui's large and solid cairn was encrusted with snow and ice. As I had carried my pipes up to the hilltop it seemed necessary to play, or attempt to play, a tune there, but one's fingers in a frost-laden wind are not at their best for executing the grace notes of a pibroch.

If the ascent of Ben MacDhui had been arduous the descent in places was still more formidable. We were without ice-axes and the strength of the recent blizzard had been such that it had swept all the new snow from the exposed slopes, leaving the old snow, which had been frozen and thawed until it was glass-like. Extreme care had to be exercised as we descended slopes which ended sometimes in rocks, sometimes in a precipice. This unorthodox winter mountaineering of a piper did not on that occasion end in disaster, and we reached, weary but intact, the hospitable home of Donald Fraser, who then lived at the Derry. I recall that when we knocked at the door and Mary Fraser opened it her first astonishment at seeing two wayfarers on a winter night was succeeded by mirth which surprised and disconcerted us. When we entered the house and stood before a mirror the cause of the merriment was apparent; we had not seen ourselves for a week and were impressive in our week's beards but the colour of our faces was still more mirth-producing for they were black from the peat smoke which had filled the bothy.

HOS-51

A DEGREE OF HELP FROM CORROUR

During the summer of 1911, a week before taking my honours degree at Oxford, I travelled up from that city to Aviemore with Malcolm Barclay Harvey, my contemporary at the University. We left on a Friday evening, reached Aviemore the following morning and were conveyed by the celebrated Mr. MacWilliam in his 'machine' to the upper bothy at Loch Eanaich. We then climbed, by the stalking path, through Coire Dhondail out onto the flat which we crossed to the shoulder of Cairntoul and then descended to the Corrour bothy. The weather had been intensely hot and I remember the *Silene acaulis* was in full flower at least a fortnight before its time. The change from Oxford to the Cairngorms was a great one and, the weather continuing fine, we spent the whole of the Sunday watching the snow buntings in their corrie. On the Monday we returned over the high tops to Loch Eanaich, seeing the mist fall lightly on the far western hills. Our friend Mr. MacWilliam was awaiting us beside Loch Eanaich and we drove down to Rothiemurchus forest where the birches were beginning to shed their leaves because of the long-continued drought. We caught the five o'clock train arriving in Oxford the next morning in time for the day's work.

Most of my friends thought I was mad to have obtained leave of absence for a long week-end so near my finals but as it turned out it was fortunate for me I did so. I was attempting to take an honours degree in the School of Natural Science, my final subject being botany. I had brought back from the Cairngorms specimens of the various alpine plants we had seen and these I showed to my tutor, learning their life histories during the week which remained before my schools. In one of the papers which was set I saw to my joy the question, 'Write as fully as possible what you know about the alpine flora of Britain'. On this question I wrote upwards of 2,500 words and it was this that gave me my 'second.' Indeed at my 'viva' I soon discovered from the questions which the examiners put to me that they considered me an authority on alpine plants and my difficulty was to cloak my ignorance so I think it can be safely said that never before has a long week-end spent on the Cairngorms just before a final school at Oxford been of such help.

5

Birds of the Heights

Many, if not most, of Seton Gordon's expeditions onto the tops were made in order to study birds like 'the great three' of ptarmigan, snow bunting and dotterel, so one piece on each of these follows plus a surprising choice to those who have not seen high-nesting common gulls at home. (They still nest at Loch nan Stuirteag above Glen Geusachan though the Gaelic name translates as black-headed gull!) Chapter 3 has already described golden eagles.

PTARMIGAN

One of the earliest birds I photographed on the nest was the ptarmigan. My first sight of these handsome birds was on Morven in Aberdeenshire and during my boyhood climbs on that hill in early summer I usually saw one or two cock ptarmigan. When they rose uttering their curious snorting cry at my feet, I was filled with excitement. I used to look hopefully for the nest where they had risen although in my heart I knew they were male birds and so most unlikely to be sitting on eggs! I never saw a hen ptarmigan in those earliest years. No doubt they were sitting close and I never had the good fortune to come across them. My greatest ambition was to discover a ptarmigan's nest; the white wings and unusual cry of this mountain bird fascinated me and I remember calling on Mr. George Simms, the veteran naturalist and taxidermist, at his shop in Aberdeen hoping that I would be able to learn about the nesting habits of the ptarmigan. Mr. Simms had seen the nests of most birds but he confessed that he had never discovered a ptarmigan's nest, although he had frequently searched. This made me more anxious than ever to find the nest; I tackled stalkers and gamekeepers but they could give me little help as their duties rarely took them up to ptarmigan ground in early summer. I knew the best ground for ptarmigan in the district where I lived and very early one morning towards the end of May I climbed the west slopes of Lochnagar, the high hill immortalized by the poet Byron. By nine o'clock in the morning I had reached a height of 3,000 feet and flushed a cock ptarmigan who flew with much croaking across a snow-filled hollow. On the farther side of this hollow he hesitated in his flight for the fraction of a second then continued on his way. I crossed the crisp snow and to my delight a hen ptarmigan fluttered from her eggs where the male bird had hesitated in his flight. The find of that nest gave me intense pleasure. I photographed the ptarmigan's eggs with care but did not attempt to photograph the bird and I believe it was the following year (1904) that I found a ptarmigan so tame that I was able to photograph her on the eggs.

Ptarmigan on occasion can be tamer than any British bird. When I was a boy an old stalker told me that he was sitting one day on a boulder on the hill eating his lunch and that after a time he noticed that the crumbs from his piece were dropping on the back of a ptarmigan sitting on her nest between his feet! Since then I have proved how close a ptarmigan can sit by approaching quietly, taking an egg from beneath her then lifting her up in my hands and setting her down again on the nest. On one occasion I three times lifted up a ptarmigan and three times placed her again on her eggs and even after that experience she remained brooding quietly.

I have sometimes played a mean trick on a mother ptarmigan. Directly the young birds are hatched the husband deserts the wife and she has all the responsibilities of rearing the brood. I have found that by imitating the shrill cheep of a young ptarmigan I am usually able to call up the mother to my feet. She imagines I have caught one of her family and creeps round me, displaying her white wings to distract my attention until she gradually realizes that the sound I am making is not *quite* like one of her own children. In 1923, a year of continued snowfalls during the latter part of May, all the high-nesting ptarmigan of the Cairngorms lost their eggs in those blizzards. The birds laid again, and were brooding their second clutches in July. Early that month my wife and I carried a hiding tent up to the Cairngorms where, at a height of 3,600 feet, we found a suitable nest of ptarmigan to photograph.

3OY-36

THE SINGER OF THE HIGH TOPS

As the July dawn strengthened on the high Cairngorms the snow bunting left his roosting crevice, shook out his feathers, and flew to his favourite boulder to salute the new day in song. His song of far-carrying bell-like notes ended in a confused whisper. As the mist curtain rose he mounted lark-like into the clear, fresh air then, in song, sailed earthward on his snow-white wings. A cock ptarmigan croaked near him and from afar came the whistle of a dotterel and the fluting of a golden plover. In damp places the starry saxifrage and the much rarer snowy saxifrage still flowered and in the corrie above him a winter snowfield lay unmelted. Through the previous night the moon had thrown a lunar rainbow across the hill pass while the snow bunting slept. At exactly two minutes past two by British Summer Time the snow bunting sang his first song. After sunrise I approached the singer sufficiently near to admire the beauty of his plumage, his white throat and head and dark bill.

Often he rose high into the air and sang as he sailed earthward with wings raised after the manner of a tree pipit. For many days I watched this songster so he lost any fear of me. Once he arrived on a stone no more than a dozen yards away and sang loudly. His beat consisted of three or four prominent boulders and a small moss-covered knoll; on this knoll he spent much of his time. He continued singing until nine o'clock in the evening. During those nineteen hours he sang, on average, three or four songs in a minute and therefore thousands during the whole period. But on one day of intense heat and sunshine he no longer sang and it was some time before I found him. I crossed to where a snowfield glistened in the sun and there I saw the bird I searched for. He was running about on the snow and often half-buried his white head in the drift; holding his head well down he would run across the drift, making a small furrow with it as though he was a miniature snow-plough. After playing this cooling and satisfying game for a time he would then fly a short distance away but soon returned to renew his pastime.

Some birds stop singing after their young are hatched. The snow bunting continued to sing until the family were on the wing. Early one morning I saw him fly down to the ground from the rock on which he had been singing and run around picking up small insects in his bill. He took wing for a short distance and then I saw a young bird appear and stand expectantly with open beak and trembling wings at the feet of its parent. The cock snow bunting at once fed this chick then I saw him feed a second member of his family. I walked to the place. The young bird he had fed first was scarcely able to fly and allowed me to approach closely and photograph it as it stood on a granite boulder. The mother bird was neither so tame or attentive as the cock but later she approached and did her best to encourage the chick to take wing by hopping beside it and encouraging it with soft, twittering notes. The young bird then became restless and flew for a short distance.

On the far side of the corrie a second snow bunting was in full song that early summer morning. The songster was easily located by his singing and he was also feeding two young birds, singing joyously as he did so. He deluded me by fluttering into the air like a skylark at the beginning of his song and swooping to the ground with a flood of fluting music, easily heard at a distance of half a mile.

The snow bunting's life, even in summer, is a hard one and during any summer month it must be prepared to face snowfall or even drifting snow which may chill its eggs and bring death to the young. On the rare fine day its discomforts must be forgotten in the joy of life high on the roof of Scotland. We do not know how far a bird can see. Small birds may not be long-sighted but the human eye sees from the snow bunting's haunt a view which remains long in the memory. Overhead, the bunting may at times see a golden eagle pass or soaring without effort, on fine days in early June swifts, flying high, may pass on their migration, it hears the croaking of ptarmigan and, rarely, the hoarse, deep bark of a passing raven. A hind and her calf may wander up to snow bunting ground but the stags are usually far below on the grassy flats where golden plover pipe. The snow bunting never hears a curlew, but sometimes the deep-toned, excited whistling of a greenshank as he 'changes over' in the deep glen far below is wafted up on the thermals. The haunts of the snow bunting give views of great beauty; I have seen in very clear weather, the twin tops of Cruachan in Argyll and, westwards, innumerable hills, one A' Faochag, *the Whelk*, from its fancied resemblance to that shellfish, rising from Glen Shiel, among the most distant. There is a tradition that the Cuillin Hills in Skye can be seen from the western Cairngorms but it has been proved by expert surveyors that this is not possible.

In spring, even as late as the first fortnight in May, one may see many snow buntings on the Cairngorms and may think that they will nest but these are birds preparing to migrate northwest to Iceland and Greenland; the Cairngorm population of nesting birds of this species is very, very small. There are seasons when the observer may search for weeks and neither hear nor see a single bird. In winter, of course, snow buntings are everywhere and may be seen along the eastern coasts of Britain from Caithness to Kent. These are travellers from the Arctic and the male birds have lost their beautiful black and white plumage of the nesting season.

HD-63

HIGH-NESTING DOTTEREL

The dotterel is the most fearless and perhaps most charming of all birds who have their homes about the high tops. So confiding is this graceful wader that in Gaelic he is known as An t-Amadan Mointeach, *the fool of the peat moss*, his absurd tameness seeming to the Highlander to mark him as a bird devoid of sense. But the dotterel is by no means a fool although his eggs would be safer from the collectors who are so often on his track were he to borrow some of the wariness and cunning of the golden plover.

The dotterel is the highest nesting bird in Britain. Wintering far to the south of these island he nevertheless chooses as a nesting ground the topmost slopes of the loftiest hills – expanses of windswept ground, too high for even the hardy ptarmigan or the elusive snow bunting. Personally, I have never come across a dotterel nesting below the 3,000-foot line, and during June, 1920, had under observation a nest at almost exactly 4,000 feet where, up to the third week in May, the winter's snow remained unbroken. Even during a fortnight in June, when in the glens beneath the air was warm and the sun shone from a cloudless sky, the wind, often gale force, was bitterly cold at this dotterel's nesting-ground.

And little wonder for a few hundred yards to the south of the nest was a great snowfield filling a wild precipitous corrie and however warm the day at lower levels, the south wind, blowing straight off the snow, brought winter in its breath. Day after day the wind had swept the plateau with gale force so that the dotterel when running about the nest in characteristic fashion had frequently to crouch low, head to wind, with legs wide apart and firmly planted on the ground till the passing of the squall.

Very early on the morning of June 10, I first located the birds. They were feeding together on a ridge 4,100 feet above sea level and for fully an hour and a half a companion [Audrey, his wife] and I watched them feed round and round us, entirely careless of our presence, even at a distance of a few yards. The morning was a magnificent one. As far as the eye could see, the deep blue fields of the sky extended without a single cloud to dim them. Only the faintest of airs stirred on the hilltop.

In the case of the dotterel the hen bird is the more brightly coloured though in this instance both cock and hen were particularly handsome. Birds nesting in the far north, or at great heights in this country, are more brightly coloured than their relatives of the south or of lower grounds. From their behaviour we were certain their nest was near but after a time both birds flew off and we saw nothing further of them that day. I was doubtful whether any bird would nest at so great a height or in so exposed a situation and came to the conclusion that this pair had lost their eggs by some mischance when nesting at lower levels and the fine morning had tempted them to this wild plateau to feed only.

Late in the evening of June 16 we again visited the plateau. Snowfields still lingered here and little growth was apparent amongst the Alpine plants although the willow of the high hills – *Salix herbacea* – was opening its minute green leaves where the snow had gone. A chill wind blew across from the snow-filled corrie to the south and in the soft evening light the plateau bore a strangely remote and desolate aspect but one of a peculiar grandeur.

After searching some likely-looking ground with little hope of success, I was delighted to see a dotterel rise just ahead of us and flutter away a few yards in characteristic manner. A short search revealed the nest, a shallow depression scraped out in a tuft of wiry hill grass and lined with dried leaves of the previous season's Alpine willow. In the nest were three beautifully marked eggs which, on being tested in some running water near, showed that they had been brooded for some days at least.

The following morning we again visited the plateau. Though the sun shone brightly, a strong cold wind swept across from the south. We had hoped to set up a hiding-tent but the force of the wind was such that the idea had to be abandoned.

The dotterel left the nest when we were still some distance away, running rapidly ahead of us. We remained silently near and it was not long before he (the male dotterel incubates the eggs) came running back in fast spurts, from time to time stopping an instant to pick up a spider or a beetle. The wind was now blowing in fierce squalls so that he had more than once to stop and hurriedly face the blast, which he did in a half-crouching, tense attitude. On one occasion he twice attempted to pick up a beetle sideways, but each time was blown away and was obliged to turn half about and make a frontal attack on his prey. On the opposite slope his mate was calling from time to time with soft whistling cries and once she passed over with swift powerful flight, swaying, however, as the gusts struck her.

From the glens far beneath the smoke from several great fires could be seen rising – for the scorching wind had now blown uninterruptedly for many days and the heather was dry as tinder. But now the weather was rapidly changing. Away to the south-west thunder clouds swiftly formed. In a very few minutes the sun was blotted out and the mutterings of thunder were heard while away westward the hills became dim and took on a curious copper-coloured appearance.

In the air was that acrid scent that so often accompanies a thunder storm and it seemed as though we should have that interesting though awe-inspiring experience of a thunderstorm actually in the clouds which were now touching the plateau. But the hills were so parched that there was no attraction for the vapours with their moisture and almost as soon as it had formed the storm passed and the sun shone out once more.

Crossing the plateau there appeared an unlooked-for visitor – a black-headed gull, a bird of the low country. Following the little burn he soon reached the top of the precipice when the wind caught him and lifted him vertically a full hundred feet before he recovered his balance.

For a dotterel, the particular bird of which I write was not tame. One had to sit no nearer than fifteen feet from the nest to ensure his returning to his eggs without delay, far warier than a dotterel we had been photographing at a height of 3,000 feet but then that bird, even for a dotterel, was absurdly confiding. From the first he showed no fear of us, allowing us to photograph him from a distance of six feet with supreme trustfulness and being obviously annoyed when, by approaching to within a foot of him we caused him to rise from his eggs and walk a yard or two away – to wait with the obvious impatience for our going. This nest was liberally lined with lichen. By June 22 the chicks were hatched out and had left the nest. But on this date the nest at 4,000 feet did not show any signs of hatching.

The fine weather had now gone from the hills. A strong southerly wind brought with it white drifting mists so it was not easy to locate the nesting ground. Plant life, refreshed by the rains, was at length stirring. The cushion pink was everywhere opening its flowers and the grasses were tingeing parts of the plateau a fresh green, good to see as a harbinger of summer.

The dotterel on this day let us approach to within a few yards when he fluttered off with tail outspread and wings drooping and quivering, all the time calling plaintively. He then disappeared into the mist but soon returned and flew straight to his eggs having, I think, lost trace of us in the clouds. We watched him awhile and after a little he few away to a grassy part of the plateau a hundred yards away where he was in the habit of feeding.

On this day, at a height of about 3,800 feet, we passed a mother ptarmigan with her brood strong on the wing and met with another family at the unusually low level – for this hill bird – of 1,800 feet. The next occasion on which the dotterel nest was visited was on June 24 – near Midsummer's Day.

For the first time since the nest was discovered it was possible to set up the hide and both my companion and I entered it. The hiding-tent was not more than twelve feet from the nest and though we entered it in full view of the dotterel he returned without suspicion and settled down confidently on the nest. He seemed, however, to find the task of hatching out his wife's eggs a dull and wearisome business and went off to feed no fewer than four times during the three hours we had him under observation. On these excursions he was away about twenty minutes at a time but on the last occasion he had already been absent from his eggs a full half-hour when we – the light having become too poor for photography – left the plateau for the day. Next morning brought mist and rain to the hill-tops but towards evening the weather cleared and the following day saw us once again at the 4,000 feet level. The nest was reached at 9.45 a.m. but the bird was off feeding and the eggs none too warm. The chicks, however, could be heard tapping vigorously on the walls of the prisons and a few minutes later Mr. Dotterel returned from his leisured meal, running rapidly over the ground and ignoring the hiding-tent which we had just erected eight feet from the nest. Even when we both sat inside the hide talking to each other in ordinary tones our presence was unnoticed. The attitude of this obligingly confiding bird seem to be 'out of sight, out of mind' for he took not the slightest notice of our conversation and several times dozed on his eggs.

Once he stood up in the nest and pecked hard at a chipping egg, apparently removing a small piece of the shell. He permitted my companion to approach to within twelve inches of him and then ran off, holding up one wing as though wounded. Once when shamming injury he shrieked aloud, but soon forgot his anxiety and began to feed unconcernedly only a few yards away, returning to the nest within ten minutes and at once falling asleep.

There was a great charm today in being on the roof of Scotland. Although the sun was hidden, the air was extraordinarily clear and, a rare thing for these altitudes, not a breath of wind stirred. Over all was a great silence, save for the distant sound of a waterfall in the corrie below and the song of a snow bunting from some neighbouring scree.

For the last time we visited the dotterel at this home amongst the clouds on June 27. The air was still on the plateau and the sun shone from a deep blue sky. What a magnificent view may be had from this wild country! From Lochnagar in the Balmoral forest, away to the conical peaks of the hills about Knoydart on the Atlantic seaboard, the shape of each hill was clear. Only on the summit of Ben Nevis clouds were resting. Away beyond the Moray Firth could be seen the blue smoke from some moor or forest fire.

On reaching the nest we found two chicks already hatched, one of them crouching about a foot outside the nest. They were quite dry and had evidently hatched out during the night or small hours of the morning; the third egg was addled.

The father dotterel appeared very pleased that his monotonous duty had been crowned with success and whenever the chicks moved under him purred with a curious though pleasing note. During the course of the morning a pair of dotterel which had apparently lost their eggs fed up close to him. He thereupon flew off the nest with feathers ruffled with anger and fiercely drove away the intruders. By midday both chicks could run actively and made excursions from the nest, returning obediently when called by their father. A little later they left the nest for good.

For some little time the parent bird was unwilling to leave the addled egg. On two or three occasions he returned to it, brooding it for a few seconds and listening intently for the tapping of a young bird. But the egg was unresponsive so he hurried back to his two chicks and, after awhile, gave up this brooding as an unprofitable business and returned to the egg no more. Although he fed a good deal himself he never made any attempt to feed his young nor to instruct them how to feed. The chicks nevertheless actively picked up minute objects and one swallowed or tried to swallow a blade of grass as long as itself.

An interesting discovery we made and which I have never seen chronicled before was that the young dotterel leave the nest, run actively, and even feed – or at all events pick up things – before their eyes are open! Indeed one of the chicks which we examined in the afternoon had even then, after several hours of wandering, its eyes still almost closed. We had noticed before that they seemed to be uncertain of their feet, frequently falling over, and stumbling against stones, but considering that their eyes at this time were still closed their movements were nothing short of marvellous.

The fine weather was of brief duration. About two o'clock the sun was obscured and grey clouds drifted in ever-increasing masses across the plateau from the southwest. One by one, the big hills to the westward were blotted out and the wind blew chill from the advancing mists.

The dotterel called his two chicks to him, for they were feeling the cold – curiously enough, the hen had never once put in an appearance even on this auspicious occasion when her family first saw the light – and made a charming picture as he brooded them in the shelter of a tiny tuft of green grass, a plant of cushion pink with rich red flowers blooming profusely only a few feet from him. And so we left him wishing him well with his family cares in that wild snow-splashed country of the high hills and dark lochans, the home of the mists and of the four winds, and where the foot of man rarely treads.

WON-21

I had taken with me a small box of worms to see whether I could induce my friendly dotterel to feed from my hand. He was so tame that when I placed my hand over the eggs he attempted to brood it; he fearlessly picked up insects two feet from me yet he took no interest in the worms I offered him and did not seem to realize they were good to eat. (Incidentally I discovered that half an hour's exposure to bright sun and cold wind killed a lively worm stone-dead.) One day he was feeling the heat and continuously panted with wide open bill. A snow bridge spanned the bed of a hill burn a few hundred yards from the nest and I brought up a large snowball which I placed a few inches to windward of him. Almost at once he stopped panting and dozed in the grateful coolness.

ISNB-41

COMMON GULL

While in most districts these handsome members of the gull family nest on the coast, in Aberdeenshire they choose as nesting sites the highest mountain tarns and rear their young with the golden eagle and ptarmigan as neighbours.

There is one lonely mountain loch I know well, lying at nearly 3,000 feet which is a favourite nesting haunt. At this altitude spring is backward and the surface of the loch is usually frozen until well on in April. Once, on the 16th of that month, while on my way to the loch, I noticed a flock of gulls flying at a great height, evidently coming from their nesting site. They were calling loudly to each other in a querulous tone and on reaching the loch I saw the reason for their disappointment: the tarn was completely ice bound and deep snowdrifts lay everywhere.

In all probability the company of gulls was an advance guard sent by the main colony to report the state of the loch and was returning with the unwelcome intelligence that it would be quite impossible to take up quarters there for some time.

The Gaelic name of the loch is Loch nan Eun (*Loch of the Birds*). As the old language has practically died out in the neighbourhood the name shows that the gulls have made the loch their home for generations.

The winter is spent on the sea coast and the gulls migrate inland early in March if the spring is favourable; until May they frequent the valleys. It is an interesting sight to see them coming down to rest after their long flight from the coast. Arriving at a great height, they reconnoitre carefully before descending in a body at some favourite locality which affords a wide outlook.

Their nesting season is late and few of the gulls commence to brood till the last days of May and, if anything, they are later nesters than ptarmigan. The usual nesting site is on a little knoll at the edge of a loch and if there are any prominent boulders the gulls generally place their nests on these. A favourite site is on a large stone some little distance out in the water where they are comparatively secure from the attacks of foxes, stoats, and other enemies.

The eggs number two, sometimes three, occasionally only one. They are large for the size of the bird and are beautifully coloured, being of an olive green spotted and blotched with dark brown; but the ground colour and markings vary considerable. A scanty nest is constructed, usually a few pieces of dry grass while sometimes a hollow is scraped by the hen and the eggs deposited without any attempt at nest-making.

During the period of incubation the male bird is constantly on the look-out and may be seen soaring in the vicinity of the nest. Once from the top of a precipice, I was watching a pair of gulls on a tiny loch below, the hen sitting on her nest on an islet and the cock flying about and calling loudly in a most dissatisfied manner. I was anxious to find out the cause of this discontent so lay perfectly quiet. Soon a herd of deer, which had been grazing out of sight, came trotting contentedly down to the edge of the loch eager for the cool water, for the day was very warm. All through the month of June large snow-fields were lying round the loch and on these many deer, both stags and hinds, were lying half asleep. As the deer entered the water, at no point more than a few feet deep, the hen gull rose from the nest and through my binoculars I could clearly make out the two eggs. Both birds sailed angrily around the deer, calling loudly, "Kick, kieu, kieu, kieu," and evidently causing the latter no little anxiety as they soon left the water. One solitary individual persisted in browsing at the edge of the loch after his fellows had moved away. The male gull stood it for some time but at length losing all patience, made an angry swoop at the startled animal which did not stop to argue but fled in a dazed way – whereupon the gull settled on a rock and visibly swelled with importance, receiving the congratulations of his mate.

An added charm is afforded the ornithologist who studies these interesting birds in their summer haunts, his only companions besides the gulls being the beautiful ptarmigan and the lordly golden eagle, with an occasional absurdly confiding dotterel. The view from these mountains is unsurpassed, and on a clear day, from the *Loch of the Birds* the river Dee – from here only a tiny stream – is seen dashing down Brae Riach's giant precipice, a distance of perhaps twenty miles away.

I think the common gull and the golden eagle are on quite friendly terms and even if an eagle should take it into his head to try to catch a gull he would have a difficult task as the gull's soaring powers are nearly as good as his own. The male gull is very pugnacious and will attack anything that ventures near his nesting site. At the hands of a colony of these birds a fox has a very bad time and, on one occasion I watched, from a distance of over a mile, a goosander swimming and diving in the vicinity of a stone on which a gull was perched. I felt pretty sure that the latter would not stand this long and sure enough when the goosander swam close past the stone the gull swooped at him in a fury and effectually banished him from that part of the loch.

The young gulls are hatched out by the latter part of June but some do not leave the shell till July. They take to the water almost immediately they are hatched and are very carefully looked after by the parent birds. While the intruder is yet a long way off one gull is seen to leave the loch and make for him with strong wing-beats, then another rises, and another, and the air is filled with wailing cries as the gulls rise in a body.

One day last July I visited the loch to try to obtain some photographs of the young birds at home. On arriving I found one pair of gulls especially demonstrative, swooping at me repeatedly, and then I noticed two tiny youngsters, only an hour or so old, floating behind a large rock in the centre of the loch where they had evidently been hatched. Although able to float perfectly, they found it impossible to swim against the waves and were gradually carried to the shore. As there was little cover for them to hide in, I thought I was fairly sure to get a successful photograph but one hid so effectually that I could find no trace of it and, on the wind dropping, the other made for the loch again. So, as the parent birds were in a great state of anxiety I left them in peace. These were an exceptionally late brood as often by the third week in July there is scarcely a gull left on the loch.

Late in the nesting season, when the young have learned to take care of themselves to a certain extent, the adult gulls sometimes leave the loch for hours on end and may be heard in the quiet of the evening noisily flying up to their nesting haunt.

The young birds when fully fledged are of a dark brown colour, even darker than a curlew, and would certainly not be taken for gulls by the novice. For some weeks they remain in the valleys near where they were hatched but by the end of August both young and old have left for the coast where they will remain until the voice of spring calls them once more to the mountains.

BLM-07

Another change is in the habits of the common gull and the black-headed gull. The common gull is now nesting on two high lochs where previously it was unknown: Loch Etchachan, 3,100 feet (usually frozen until well into May) and Loch nan Stuirteag, between Braeriach and Monadh Mor. Even as recently as thirty years ago there were no seagulls nesting on these mountain lochs.

The black-headed gull has formed the new habit of flying up to the highest hills almost daily. It may be seen feeding on the black mountain moths of the Braeriach plateau at 4,000 feet, beside the Wells of Dee. The moths suck the nectar from the blossoms of the cushion pink which beautify the Braeriach plateau at midsummer.

Before the first war it was rare to see a black-headed gull here. Another bird which has moved up comparatively recently to nest on the Cairngorms is the lapwing, which in places nests actually in ptarmigan country.

HS-71

6

Cairngorm – Macdhui – Loch Avon

This area may be regarded as the heart of the Cairngorms, taking in the heights and depths between Lairig Ghru and Lairig an Laoigh. It seemed appropriate to have Cairngorm reached from Glen More and Macdhui from Glen Derry, routes most visitors will follow and everyone at some time should spend a night under or beside the Shelter Stone. Years ago I was there with some youngsters who found a visitors' book in the shelter. We laughed at one entry: 'It moved!'

CAIRNGORM FROM GLENMORE

One day in late March a friend and I drove to Aviemore from the south. The mist was low on the hills of Drumochter and wet snowflakes were falling on the white plumage of the whooper swans that fed on Loch Alvie. We crossed the Druie at Coylum Bridge and as we came in sight of Loch Morlich saw that, although the war was over, tree-felling operations continued. Some of the finest Scots pines which remained were now being felled and woodcutters' huts had appeared on the north shore of the loch. Wind flurries swept across Loch Morlich, a goosander rose from his fishing and flew low over the loch and from the old pines crested tits scolded and chattered huskily. To the north-west the sky cleared and showed blue above the Monadh Liath (the old name of the Cairngorm range was Am Monadh Ruadh, *the Red Hills*, as contrasted with Am Monadh Liath, *the Grey Hills)*. Cairngorm is usually climbed by the well-trodden right-of-way from Glenmore Lodge yet there is a more interesting ascent from the neighborhood of Revoan (Ruighe a' Bhothain, *Shieling of the Bothy*) some three miles along the old drove road beyond the lodge. Plantations of spruce and Douglas fir are now growing tall where the old Scots pines stood forty years ago but these ancients still rise in stately grandeur on the slopes of Meall a' Bhuachaille, *the Herdsman's Hill*, so widely spaced that the heather grows long beneath them. The track passes beside Lochan Uaine, *the Green Tarn*, whose clear waters of pale greenish-blue lie in the cold shadow of Creag nan Gall. Old pines overshadow Lochan Uaine and among them are juniper bushes which seem also of great age. Perched on one of these bushes a hedge accentor sang vigorously. The dunnock moved his head in an animated manner and threw a high-pitched, thin song, to the keen, cold air.

A short climb through long, wet heather where hailstones lay brought us to the slope which was the beginning of four miles of wind-swept ridge leading to

Loch Bhrodainn in the heart of the Pass of Gaick

Above: Loch Einich below the Sgoran Dubh hills

Left: The rushing waters of the River Beanaidh draining Gleann Einich

Seton Gordon spying the Lairig Ghru from Braeraich

Braeriach's northern corries in April; spate-carried boulders in the foreground

Left: Down to Loch Einich from Coire Dhondail

Below: On the Moine Mhor – flat-topped Cairn Toul above

Camping on the Moine Mhor

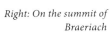

Above: Encamped on the high tops of the Cairngorms

Right: On the summit of Braeriach

Left: Seton Gordon's wife Audrey looking across to Sgor an Lochain Uaine

Below: Golden eagles and young at an eyrie

Golden eagle shielding its chick from the sun

Above: A gentle preening from a mighty eagle beak

Left: An eagle chick growing into adult plumage

Golden eagle taking off from its eyrie in a tree

The Devil's Point and smoke rising from Corrour bothy

Seton Gordon at Poll an Eisg near the meetings of Glens Geusachan and Dee

Towards the top of Lairig Ghru

Above: Into the Lairig Ghru

*Right: Seton Gordon at the
     Tailors' Stone in the
     Lairig Ghru*

Above: Seton Gordon seated at the door of Corrour bothy

Right: Seton Gordon approaching the site of a peregrine nest

A ptarmigan on her nest, taken from a hide

Importuning ravens at their nest

The nesting dotterel being cooled by a snowball kindly placed upwind

Above: The loch where the common gulls would later nest

Right: Seton Gordon photographing a dotterel from a few feet away

Sgor an Lochain Uaine

Loch Etchachan looking over Loch Avon to Cairngorm

Loch Etchachan

From Ben Macdhui across the plateau towards Cairngorm; September snowfall

At the Shelter Stone by Loch Avon

Loch Avon

Loch Morlich and the Cairngorms

the summit of Cairngorm. We could see that in the Spey valley the sun shone and lighted the snowy slopes of Ben Rinnes, but hail and snow squalls were forming over the Monadh Liath and soon one of these squalls approached. When it reached Loch Morlich it seemed to hang there without movement, as though to gather fresh energy for its assault on Cairngorm. Soon hail poured aslant upon us and drifted smoke-like across the face of the hill. The squall passed, the view was restored and for a time the sun shone from a blue sky. Two male ptarmigan in snowy winter plumage flew fast across the hill slopes. One was in strong pursuit of the other: a hen bird, the cause of the dispute, flew a short distance behind them. The ptarmigan rocked as they flew, moving at great speed at a little height above the drift that swept like smoke across those exposed slopes. Dark chocolate-coloured clouds formed to wind-ward, quickly increasing in size. Despite the strong wind they approached slowly, all the time becoming more formidable. The light faded and the mist descended on the hilltop which we were now nearing. From this Arctic twilight on Cairngorm we saw, in the direction of the Moray Firth, the sky a delicate blue and partly over-spread by the white, fleecy clouds of fair weather. Where we walked the wind was so strong that small pebbles were blown over the newly fallen snow which lay on the old snowfields, margined with solid ice where the recent thaw had begun to melt them. We walked over the snow to the accompaniment of a crunching noise; so hard was the snowy surface that our footmarks scarcely showed. We entered the cloud and followed the guiding cairns to the hilltop. We reached the large summit cairn and sheltered in its lee; the cold was intense and one's jaws were stiffened so that speech was not easy. Suddenly the mist curtain was roughly torn aside by the gale and before it was again drawn across the hilltop there was revealed a transient view of Beinn Mheadhoin, the great rocks on its summit snow-encrusted and, beyond that hill, the cold, dead-white upper slopes and plateaux of Beinn a' Bhuird and Ben A'an. During those fleeting moments a steel-blue sky showed at the zenith. More speedily than can be related, the mist-curtain once again hid the view, which had been phantom-like and grand in the extreme. The wind increased with the mist and the snow drifted more densely.

That evening beside Loch Morlich the curlews were silent except for an occa-sional long-drawn melancholy whistle, low-toned and plaintive. Towards sunset the squalls of hail and snow became more dense and drew closer on the Monadh Liath. Cuithe Crom, the snow bed on Cairngorm, reflected on its white expanse the pearl-grey of the sky, and the old pines were darkly reflected in the waters of Loch Morlich as the first star shone out. Roding woodcock flitted across the forest clearings.

A summer climb on Cairngorm at the end of June gave us strange varieties of weather. At midnight the low moon, rising golden behind the long ridge west of Cairngorm summit, gave the illusion of sunrise. When the sun did shine, the light was very clear but before we had begun the climb dark thunder clouds had formed above the Monadh Liath and it could be seen that torrential rain was falling on those hills. The curlew were now in full song and oystercatchers piped shrilly beside Loch Morlich. The climb beneath the midsummer sun was more tiring than under the wintry conditions of March. The area had recently been acquired by the state as a Forest Park. Below Glenmore Lodge [the present youth hostel] was a notice CAMPING GROUND, and here were parked motor-cars and a number of small tents. One party had erected a rain-proof passage between car and tent, a wise precaution.

We left the path at 3,500 feet and crossed the short alpine herbage to look down at the pocket of snow in Ciste Mhearad (*Margaret's Chest*). The snow often remains here throughout the year and by late summer has become stained by peat dust and almost as hard as ice. Here dwarf cudweed grows to the edge of the snow but at the lowest level of the hollow there is no plant life; the period of exposure to sun and air is too short to support any.

One of the highest wells on the Cairngorms is not far from this snow-holding pocket, the Marquis's well, said to have received its name from the Marquis of Argyll who was defeated at the battle of Glen Livet in or about the year 1594. There is also an Argyll Stone on Sgoran Dubh. It is more likely that the well is named after the Marquess of Huntly for at the time of the battle of Glen Livet Argyll was an Earl not a Marquis. A short distance south-east of Cairngorm summit is an outcrop of rock from which Loch A'an can be seen 1,500 feet below, the river A'an flowing from it. On this June day a dark thunder cloud was creeping up from the east and threatening to envelop the hilltop as we looked down on the loch. On Ben MacDhui snow gleamed above the bed of the Garbh Uisge which dropped in a white cascade to the head of Loch A'an. To the westward, we could see the figures of men standing on the summit of Braeriach. The cloud now pressed on over the plateau and the hilltop where we stood began to steam. Behind us a small rainbow appeared, and the hilltop assumed a peculiar beauty during the few short minutes before the cloud finally covered it and hid the sun. When the rain which fell turned to sleet and a lifting of cloud westward showed the storm was passing we came upon a hen ptarmigan with a very young brood. She was near the Cuithe Crom which was still extensive and so hard that one could with difficulty cross it by reason of its hard snow and steepness of slope; even Dugie the collie hesitated to run down it.

HOS-51

The area changed rapidly; twenty years later he reflected as follows. What would he write today one wonders?

Many more people now visit the Cairngorms. A good road has been made from Loch Morlich to the shoulder of Cairngorm (4,084 feet). This new road allows motorists to drive to a height of rather more than 2,000 feet. Thence, in six and a half minutes, one is transported by chairlift to within 300 feet of the summit of Cairngorm. It is curious to feel the air temperature swiftly drop during the ascent and to be deposited on a plateau high above the heather line where the Arctic willow (*Salix herbacea*) takes its place. I was told that a ptarmigan had nested within three feet of where men were at work erecting a snow fence. Despite much hammering and human activity, the brooding bird sat tight and hatched her chicks.

When the approach road and the chairlift were visualized, many people feared that much of the charm of the Forest of Glenmore and Cairngorm itself would be destroyed but the road is already harmonizing with the scenery, and the chairlift enables thousands of skiers to enjoy their pastime on the high slopes from late autumn until the following summer. Last year in early July men and women were still skiing on large snowfields.

Near the head of Coire Cas, a north-facing corrie is a great snowbed that is a summer landmark from distant hills, such as Morven in Caithness. It is one of the few snowfields in Scotland that carry a name and is called Cuithe Crom, *the Bent Snow Wreath*, because it is in the form of a sickle. This great snowbed survived the heatwave of early June and still loomed vast at the edge of the clouds when I saw it six weeks later.

The chair-lift on Cairngorm give a Continental atmosphere to the place; it did not, therefore, seem surprising to see a reindeer being fed on sandwiches by tourists. I pictured to myself the amazement with which the old deerstalkers of a past generation would have witnessed the scene. The chairlift, too, has altered the bird life of Cairngorm. In summer the black-headed gulls that nest in colonies on Strathspey have found that the discarded remains of many lunches and teas eaten by visitors provide an easy food supply. At the car park the gulls stand in rows, or fly overhead. We saw them later performing aerobatics high above the summit of Cairngorm. [Migrant snowbunting also visit the car parks of our ski resorts, hopping among cars like sparrows.]

Even in this late July it was possible to find *Silene acaulis*, the cushion pink, still in bud and I have now had the unusual experience of finding it in flower in three consecutive months. At the beginning of May, when the Cairngorms were still under deep snow, there were cushions in full blossom near the sea in the north wing of the Isle of Skye; a month later it added a touch of colour on Beinn Storr on the same island and now, late in July, the rosy flowers were attracting the hardy black

Alpine moths to sip their honey. It was even more unusual to find the pink china-like flowers of the Alpine azalea (*Loiseleuria procumbens*) on the gravelly ridges as in a warm season it is usually in flower early in June.

HS-71

MACDHUI FROM THE DERRY

Ben Muich Dhui, *The Hill of the Black Sow* or *MacDuff's Hill*, 4,296 feet, was long supposed to be the highest mountain in Great Britain, but now Ben Nevis, 4,406 feet, has been given the place of honour. In late August, when the grass and blaeberry covering their slopes are still at their best, the high hills have always a great charm. Leaving Braemar early in the morning, we have a delightful drive up Glen Lui but tyre troubles bring our car to a standstill and a good deal of valuable time is lost. In the glen we pass a very old tramp whom we take to be a Russian and who informs us with pride that he has come through the Lairig from Aviemore and a little farther on we meet two kilted stalkers on their way down to Braemar. Although the barometer is high and rising, the morning is none too promising away to the west. On the Cairngorms the mist is rising and falling and as we near the Derry we see Monadh Mor dimly through haze but as we walk up Glen Derry the weather improves and the sun shines strongly. Burns are exceptionally low but in spite of the continued drought the hill-sides are wonderfully green and the deer are grazing contentedly. For some time we have a very fine view of Ben Mheadhoin, *The Middle Hill*, with the early morning mist resting on its slopes and the rocks on the summit rising above the cloud. The heather on the low grounds is in full bloom and the scent is delicious.

Up to this point we have followed the Lairig an Laoigh, *the Calves Pass*, which crosses to Abernethy in the sister valley of the Spey but now we turn westward and head up Choire Etchachan, keeping near the burn. The head of Choire Etchachan is a favourite haunt of the ptarmigan and they are almost certain to be found here at every season. The golden eagle, too, is often seen in the corrie and I have watched a pair playing with each other above the summit of Ben Mheadhoin. Loch Etchachan, lying at a height of 3,100 feet, is the highest loch of any importance in Great Britain.

Concerning the derivation of the word there seems to be a great deal of uncertainty, some hold it is a corruption of Aitaonach – *abounding in juniper* – and, as there are a good many bushes of this shrub in the vicinity, this may be correct. As we reach the top of the corrie we have a magnificent view of the loch, deep blue in the morning sun, with Ben Muich Dhui in the background. The hill as yet carries a good deal of snow and one drift in a corrie immediately east of the summit very rarely disappears. The corrie is known as the Snowy Corrie and to-day, so far as we can measure, the snow is at least 60 feet in depth.

Instead of following the path straight to the summit we turn north and make for the Shelter Stone and Loch Avon. Before us we have Cairngorm, 4,084 feet, with the morning's mist enveloping the summit and at times Ben Muich Dhui is mist-capped also. All at once we reach the edge of the plateau and look down on Loch Avon, 2,400 feet. This loch lies in a deep trough, bounded to the north by Cairngorm, west by Ben Muich Dhui, and south by Ben Mheadhoin. It is over a mile in length and exceedingly deep. From the loch issues the Water of Avon which enters the Spey at Ballindalloch. Leaving the plateau overlooking the loch we descend to the Shelter Stone where many mountaineers spend the night before scaling Ben Muich Dhui. We reach the Feith Bhuidhe (as the Avon is called before it enters Loch Avon) a little way west of the loch and from here strike up the steep hill-side to the summit of Ben Muich Dhui, following the burn all the way. All around the loch blue-bells [the Scot's harebell] are met with in great profusion, and we do not remember ever having seen flowers of so large a size.

The day is now intensely hot with only a slight breeze from the west so we make some tea about half-way up the Feith Bhuidhe and afterwards push on refreshed. We soon reach the snow which had been drifted along the plateau during the winter. At one point we come upon the remains of an avalanche, a day or two old, and huge blocks of snow, some over six feet high, lie scattered about the hillside, looking as though they had been cut with some gigantic spade. In places the snow has carried down pieces of rock and here we find a small Cairngorm stone. The great heat of the sun is having its effect on the snow which is quickly melting and streams of water are issuing from the drifts. We come upon a hen ptarmigan which is most confiding and we see her brood of well-grown youngsters sunning themselves a few yards away. Some are half-asleep on stones, others are walking lazily about, but they pay little attention to us. The plateau reached, we find the summit still some distance away and the walking, too, is very bad at this point but we keep close to the burn and leave it only a few hundred yards from where it rises. Bird life is scarce at this height but we see a few meadow pipits and a solitary peregrine flies past, making towards Braeriach.

The summit cairn of Ben Muich Dhui is reached about 3.30 p.m., and although the day is very fine we have no distant view owing to the haze. Aviemore is made out and, westward, Braeriach and Cairntoul across the valley of the Dee. The Garbh-choire burn is seen threading its way down from Braeriach like a line of silver and we also note the Devil's Point, 3,303 feet, and the Angel's Peak on Cairn Toul, so named, it is said, to keep the demon in his place. After leaving the summit we have some glissading in the Snowy Corrie and a little farther hear the call-note of the snow bunting and flush a covey of ptarmigan. As we descend Coire Etchachan the sun is sinking behind Ben Muich Dhui and the deer are returning to the low grounds for the night while the few grouse which the golden eagle has left [unscattered] are calling loudly in the evening calm. As we reach the Derry darkness is fast coming on and the last glow of the sunset is sinking behind Ben Bhrotain and Monadh Mor.

COH-12

THE SHELTER STONE OF LOCH A'AN

Loch A'an (Gaelic, Loch Ath-fhinn) is the greatest loch of the high Cairngorms, cradled in the bosom of the hills, 2,400 feet above sea-level and May has arrived before its clear waters are released by the ice. Great hills guard Loch A'an well: northward, Cairngorm rises almost sheer, to the south are the steep rocky slopes of Beinn Mheadhon, west, stands the vast bulk of Ben MacDhui. It is difficult to see Loch A'an, even from the high ground of the Cairngorms, and perhaps the best viewpoint is the head of that magnificent Alpine corrie which rises to Ben MacDhui from the western shore of the loch.

One July morning of intense heat, when the thermometer at Aviemore was standing at 82°F, a companion and I climbed from Rothiemurchus forest, where blaeberries in their thousands were already ripe and the ling was almost in blossom, by way of Creag an Leth-choin and Lochan Buidhe to the great tableland that extends from Ben MacDhui to Cairngorm. Clouds had hidden the sun but we reached the plateau and a warm southerly breeze was bringing refreshing rain to the hills. Red deer are quick to climb to the high ground when there is pasture for them and a herd of perhaps 150 stags were feeding beside Lochan Buidhe. Many of the hinds had young claves beside them and the soft, high-pitched bleating of the fawns (a sound not unlike the mewing of cats) mingled with the deeper cries of the mothers as they answered.

We walked east over the green carpet of minute Arctic willow and as we reached the edge of the plateau looked down into dark Loch A'an encircled by black cliffs. We stood at the head of a corrie through which the water known as Geur Uisge Beag (or Garbh Uisge Beag) flows to the loch. Beneath us was a huge snow-field of great depth. Despite the heat, the surface of the snow was icy-hard for it had been frozen and thawed alternately for many months. At the edge of the snow the grass was brown, a few yards away it was already green and in vigorous growth. Beside the snow a wheatear stood, near it a pair of meadow pipits were flying.

Beneath us a heavy thundershower formed and grew and drew a veil before Loch A'an. At the passing of the shower the sky was blue and in the heavens were piled up great thunder clouds on which the evening sun shone golden. Beneath us Geur Uisge Beag mingled its waters with those of a sister stream, Geur Uisge Mor, having its source beneath one of the largest snowfields of the Cairngorms, a short distance north-east of Ben MacDhui summit. This field of snow was melting so rapidly that Geur Uisge Mor was a torrent of foaming waters. We followed these waters to the cliff edge and saw them leap to Loch A'an in a series of splendid waterfalls.

By descending a little distance to the north of these falls it is possible to walk down to Loch A'an and its Shelter Stone without difficulty, through a great corrie (curiously, unnamed on any map) that must surely be the finest in all the Cairngorm range. In this corrie three streams of considerable size meet. They are the Geur Uisge Mor, the Feith Bhuidhe, and the white foaming burn which drains Coire Domhain of Cairngorm. In the corrie are many Alpine plants: July violets which mingle their flowers of intense blue with those of the butterwort, in the spray of the falls are the pale petals of the starry saxifrage, and here and there are plants of the globe flower and the harebell. At a height of 2,700 feet I passed a raspberry bush.

It was evening when we reached the foot of the corrie. We looked back in the soft light at a scene of grandeur. Over the rocks at the head of the corrie the Feith Bhuidhe flowed invisible beneath a great snowfield, the waters emerging from an arch of snow then hurrying onward in a foaming tumult to where Loch A'an serenely awaited their coming – and quietened their youthful eagerness. From a precipice south of the loch great rocks in a past age have been hurled and lie in confusion beneath the parent cliff. One enormous boulder rests upon several others in such a manner that a recess or hollow capable of sheltering and concealing a number of persons has been formed. This is the celebrated Clach Dion or *Shelter Stone*, which for centuries has been used as a sleeping place by hunters and, more recently, by lovers of the high and solitary places of the Cairngorms. As we reached the Shelter Stone the air was warm and still, perfumed by the young shoots of crowberry.

The Shelter Stone stands at 2,500 feet and the Alpine vegetation surrounding it is unusually luxuriant. Blaeberry plants here were taller than those of the same species in Rothiemurchus Forest. The berries in the sun-heated forest were already ripe, here they were small and green. Mingled with them were plants of the great blaeberry, distinguished by their glaucous leaves and more woody stems. This plant rarely flowers or fruits in the Cairngorms but the unusually warm summer had encouraged the production of a few blossoms and berries. Around the great boulder was a carpet of cloudberries with many fruits already large and red which, when ripe, become almost yellow.

Close to the Shelter Stone lay Loch A'an, opal-tinted in the soft evening light. Many small trout were rising on its windless waters; their rings crossed and re-crossed one another. That night at ten o'clock we sat beside the sandy bay where the hill torrent entered the loch and in the crystal clear water saw many trout and every few seconds one would rise to the surface to suck down some small fly or midge. One very dark trout in its wanderings apparently entered the territory of his neighbour for a light-colour trout vigorously drove the trespasser away. At half-past ten, as twilight was deepening, a goosander flew up quietly and alighted with a splash in the sandy estuary of the stream. She had failed to observe us and after preening her feathers awhile began to fish. With stealthy movements, throwing her head forward at each stroke of her webbed feet, she cruised around, and the trout, seeing her, hurried into deeper water. Once she made a sudden rush but it was too dark to see whether she caught a fish. A little later, when she was close to us, a trout unsuspectingly swam near her. We were sure she would capture it but it easily escaped and then she rose from the loch and was quickly lost to sight in the dusk.

Beside the Shelter Stone was the small earth of a fox. A cock grouse, rising from the dew-drenched heather, broke the silence with his cheery becking. The interior of the Shelter Stone on so fine and warm a night was dark and depressing so we chose for our couch a narrow, heathery shelf out in the open, protected from dew and rain by an overhanging corner of the great stone. On this shelf we lay during the short hours between sunset and sunrise with the noise of falling waters in our ears and the peace and silence of the great hills about us.

Many persons have passed a night beneath the Shelter Stone. The Prime Minister, Mr. Ramsay MacDonald, who is a great walker and hill lover, gave me an interesting account of his experience there. Readers may know of the tragedy of New Year 1933 when two climbers incautiously passed a midwinter night below that great stone. On their return over Cairngorm to Aviemore they were overtaken by a winter blizzard of great severity and both died in the snow beside the burn of Coire Cas – with the worst of their journey behind them.

At midnight the sky was clear and a star burned in the depths of Loch A'an. At one o'clock thin mists began to form on the slopes of Beinn Mheadhon. These mists grew stealthily and by sunrise Loch A'an was hemmed in by billowing cloud. An hour later this cloud reached us so we were shut in by a grey, motionless vapour that deadened the murmur of the waterfalls above us. There was no chill in the air and we remained on our hard couch in the hopes that the clouds would lift before midday. We were not disappointed. Shortly after eleven o'clock the sharp summit of the great cliff known as the Sticil, which rises almost sheer from the Shelter Stone, loomed grandly through the cloud and gradually the whole precipice, dark and grim even on this summer morning, stood revealed. A narrow gully in the cliff was still filled with snow, and high up on the precipice was a curious circular hollow which called to mind Ossian's Cave in Glencoe.

The air everywhere was clearing. In soft woolly balls the clouds hung on the side of the snowy corrie of the Geur Uisge then gradually dissolved. Shortly before noon we left the Shelter Stone. A pair of meadow pipits were courting beside the stone and the sun was now faintly seen above the upper clouds. The Geur Uisge had shrunk in size (at night the snows melt more slowly) and we crossed without difficulty. The air was sultry as we climbed the steep corrie and reached the snow. Although the season was mid-July the blaeberry plants were not yet in flower at the edge of the snow and the Alpine ferns, imprisoned below the snow for many months, were only now beginning to unroll their fronds. Violets were in bud or in flower and here and there a cushion of draba (rock cress) grew on the damp rocks.

While we were climbing the corrie the mists had collected into a dense cloud above Loch A'an and now, floating up into the corrie, they pressed in on us so that we walked through dense vapours. We followed Geur Uisge Beag until we had reached a height by aneroid of 3,500 feet above the sea, then turned north towards Feith Bhuidhe. Soon a wall of snow towered almost vertically above us, its top invisible in cloud. Along the foot of this great snow wall we groped our way hearing as we walked the crying of many hinds and their calves, near but hidden in the mist. By compass and aneroid we steered for Cairn Lochan (the western outpost of Cairngorm and just under 4,000 feet) and as we reached it we emerged above the mist. We looked back across a sea of cloud to where the dark cone of Lochnagar and the rocks of Ben A'an rose above the mist. West, the mist-ocean flowed in upon Brae Riach. All the low country was hidden and we looked instead upon a vast ocean of mist gently stirring in places as a light eddy of air played upon it.

Late that day, as we crossed Creag an Leth-choin and looked into the misty depths of the Lairig Ghru, a mutter of thunder came from a black cloud high above us to the east. We felt it strange to walk across this lonely country with black thunder clouds high in the heavens and dun-coloured clouds far beneath us. A swift was hawking for insects above the sea of mist and although rain was falling the still air was very warm. In the mist we made our way and found in the Lairig twilight gloom an air temperature at least ten degrees lower than on the high tops. The mist had dropped so low that even the forest of pines was hidden in it and that evening, as we shivered before a fire in the Spey valley, we pictured the hinds and their calves grazing above the clouds in summer warmth on the lonely plateau of Ben MacDhui.

IOW-33

7

Birds of the Lower Grounds

Bird watching is so satisfying because it can be indulged anywhere anytime. Seton Gordon's interest was set off as a boy by the birds in his Deeside garden and, as an old man, what he then observed from his house windows in Skye was described quite as enthusiastically. Just being there, observant, reaps the rewards. Several times I've seen blackcock leks because I chanced to pitch a tent in the right place. Seton Gordon made everywhere the right place (Wasn't one of his books called Seagulls in London?*). What a pity he can't see the continuation of the osprey story as he knew it or know about the sea eagles and kites.*

ODD OYSTERCATCHERS

On a Highland river I recently had the pleasure of watching a strangely plumaged oystercatcher. A friend had written to tell me it had returned for the seventh season in succession. One spring morning of bright sunshine we set out to locate the bird. In the old forest a greater spotted woodpecker was hammering upon a tree, the noise resembling the blows of a riveter on the hull of some vessel. The lesser spotted woodpecker, a bird no larger than a chaffinch is unknown in the Highlands but the greater spotted woodpecker is widely distributed, though nowhere common. The original race became extinct more than a century ago but new arrivals have since populated many of the forests. To return to the oystercatcher. We searched for him everywhere without success and were on the point of abandoning our quest when a fisherman told us he had seen the bird in a field and we found him feeding by himself a little apart from several paired birds. In the normal plumaged oystercatcher the head, throat and back are jet-black. In this individual the head and throat are almost pure white, the white feathers extending a little way along the back. Round either eye is a circle of dark feathers. This considerable white area is faintly mottled with black.

After feeding upon worms for a time he flew across the river and, when at a considerable height, changed the usual rapid wing beats to the slow, gull-like flaps that are associated with the song. From this I judged it to be a male. He has been seen incubating the eggs but both male and female undertake that task. Before we left the river we saw the oystercatcher again dozing on a stone on a shingle bed, his head tucked away beneath his feathers. He awoke and walked leisurely away, the sun shining on his ruby eye, his yellow bill and his white head. His mate had apparently not arrived for he was by himself.

It is a sad commentary on the baseness of some people that 'a man with a gun' should be after this beautiful and unusual bird. He has been warned off the estate and it is to be hoped his plans miscarry and that this unusual oystercatcher may return for many more seasons to the shingle beds beside the swiftly flowing river where in spring birch and larch scent the air and the missel thrush from the highest tree sings his defiant song.

A correspondent who heard of this white-headed oystercatcher has written to me to say that several summers before, in Strathspey, he saw, among a flock of oyster-catchers on the wing, a pure white individual. It may have been an albino and albinos are, I believe, rarely fertile but the oystercatcher I have described nests each season.

HY-44

DEADLY SNOWS

March 1930 was memorable because of its cold, snowy weather. The snow lay unbroken until the last week of the month and the frost had entered so deeply into the ground that some upland farmers were unable to turn a furrow between January and April. March blizzards came after curlews, lapwings and oystercatchers had arrived at their upland breeding stations. Day succeeded day yet the country remained snow-bound and all the ground-feeding birds were in desperate plight. In Upper Strath Spey the oystercatcher I think was the worst sufferer but on the mid reaches of the river the mortality among lapwings was equally great.

A correspondent paints a striking picture of the plight of the birds in his district during the storm. 'Here alone my fishermen and I picked up over two hundred birds, mostly lapwings, but among them a number of oystercatchers and curlews. One morning as I fished the Spey I counted in a quarter of an hour eighteen lapwings float past me lifeless and I subsequently found thirty-eight dead at a well. In fact all the ditches contained dead birds. I fed four oystercatchers on raw meat on my doorstep for a week. When the lapwings had become so weak that they could not fly I caught eight of them and put them in a room with a radiator. For a bed I gave them grass and fed them on raw meat. Four lived and when the snow had gone I released them in the sunshine and they flew away. One day (March 23) I picked up nine lapwings, two oystercatchers, and one curlew. For about three days after the storm there was deadly silence over field and river.'

Is it not remarkable that oystercatchers, curlews and lapwings should remain gallantly at their upland nesting grounds and rub shoulders with death? An hour's flight would take most of them back to the coast where they would find food in plenty. My own opinion is that the birds do not return to the coast because it is a strange land to them. Their coastal winter haunts, in all probability, lie hundreds of miles to the south and south-west of their nesting grounds and thus it would be against their instinct to fly down the rivers to the nearest coastline. But birds are creatures of joy and, in the surge of spring life, the survivors of snow and frost soon forgot their hardships. Less than a week after the storm the curlews were making liquid music above the heather and a pair of oystercatchers had renewed their claim to their last year's territory. The golden eagle paid little heed to the severity of the March weather and as early as the 16th I saw an eagle brooding her two eggs when the surrounding country was deep in snow.

ITH-31

EARLY BIRDS

In March the first summer migrants reach the highlands. The wheatear usually arrives at its windswept moorland haunt about the 26th. He is hard and cheerful and is able to stand a short-lived snowstorm. When he arrives he sees only two plants of the hills in flower, the purple mountain saxifrage and the draw moss.

The lapwing nests numerously along upper Strath Spey but leaves in autumn. It arrived one year at its nesting grounds at Gaick, 1,500 feet above sea level, as early as January but was quickly banished by frost and snow. The lapwing is a migratory bird and the longest flight on record was by a flock of lapwings which crossed the Atlantic (favoured by easterly gales) to Newfoundland.

East and west the habits of the oystercatcher differ. In the west the 'Bird of Saint Bride' nests beside the sea, in the east the oystercatcher is an inland bird, nesting on most of the great Scottish rivers from estuary to source. In the Forest of Gaick the oystercatchers are very tame in March. They are often recovering from recent snowfalls which have cut off their food supplies. Gaick is one of the highest shooting lodges in Scotland. Hills rise steeply from the lodge and during a winter storm great snow cornices are formed above the corries and sometimes break away as avalanches. A few years ago an avalanche descended to the birch wood near the lodge. A herd of stags were sheltering there and the snow, falling upon them, killed eleven stags, a fox, and a hare.

ITH-31

FIGHTING BLACKCOCK

One December 28 I visited a lek (fighting ground) of the blackcock. The black-cock is a cheery fellow and he works off his super-abundance of energy in an early morning tourney upon some favourite knoll where he meets his fellows. The birds are unaffected by frost and snow and even in mid-winter jauntily assemble at dawn on their fighting-ground. This knoll is usually out on the open moor, within easy flighting distance of a forest of Scots fir or birch where they roost.

The moon, near full, was shining on the snowy hills and glens as I walked over the moor shortly before seven o'clock in the morning. The air was still and seventeen degrees of frost were binding the lochs and burns. I reached the black-cocks' fighting ground as the first pale green light of dawn was contending with the moonlight glow on the horizon. I crept below a piece of canvas and lay quietly, perhaps twenty yards from the hill, to await the arrival of the combatants. Daylight strengthened and I had begun to fear the blackcock in the Arctic weather should be in no mood for sport when there was a whir of wings and a score of blackcock flew up. They alighted beside me and since I was well hidden had no suspicions. They spread out their tails and at once began to spar. The moon shining upon their white tail coverts (spread fanwise) caused a pale lemon glow, very striking and beauti-ful. Each bird selected a sparring partner. They then faced up to one another, each pair of opponents treading lightly and delicately like trained boxers waiting the psychological moment. When that moment came the birds rushed in and struck at one another with feet and bill. Breaking away without much damage done they renewed the attack or, tiring of one another, sought a fresh antagonist. They called out their challenge, springing into the air, striking their wings briskly against their sides, and uttering a sharp hissing cry.

The whole business of fighting and sparring lasted not more than fifteen minutes and then the blackcock fed for some time indolently around their fighting-ground. An old cock grouse loudly greeted the December day and the blackcock flew back to the trees where they had slept.

The fighting of the blackcock in spring is well known as is generally associated with the selection of mates but mid winter fighting has not been observed so frequently.

ITH-31

NESTING GREENHSHANK

The greenshank is one of the most wary of British birds, even the curlew is tame in comparison, as is the wild and unapproachable golden plover. Thus photographing a greenshank at her nest is difficult and calls for a large amount of patience and perseverance. During a recent season a companion and I spent a month in a wild country of bog, heather and ancient pine forest, where several pairs of greenshank have their home.

Unlike the redshank, which remains in the British Isles throughout the year, the greenshank at the close of summer migrates south, and does not put in an appearance at its nesting haunts until late March or early April. On May 10 we arrived at the nesting ground. On the high hills the snow lay unbroken, the birches leafless as in midwinter.

The greenshanks had apparently just commenced to sit, for on the loch side were solitary birds feeding – presumably the cocks. For four days we searched the most likely nesting places from morning to night without success. The weather during this time was cold and rough and we had begun to despair but on the afternoon of the 14th, while we were sitting near a loch where all the greenshanks of the district fed, one of them, rising from his dinner, flew, calling, across the forest near us, and disappeared a few hundred yards away, having evidently dropped to the ground. We surmised a nest must be near and on reaching the spot, which had been by no means easy to mark, the greenshank rose, settled for a moment, obviously surprised at our sudden appearance, then took wing uttering anxious cries. A very careful search was made over all the neighbouring ground and at length we were rewarded by finding the hen greenshank sitting on her nest. Although we were not more than six feet away the bird crouched flat and absolutely motionless on her eggs, relying on her wonderful protective colouring and evidently thinking she was invisible to our eyes. The nesting site was under a large dead pine branch, the nest being placed amongst some of the small side branches. Four eggs, handsomely coloured and marked, were in the nest, in appearance quite distinctive and unlike those of any other wader.

The following afternoon a hiding tent was erected some little distance from the nest but on returning to the spot next day we found two collectors on the ground searching for greenshanks' nests. After a slight brush, on our explaining that we had already found a nest and wished to photograph the sitting bird, the collectors transferred their energies elsewhere.

But the following morning – May 17 – on reaching the greenshanks' nesting ground, we found the nest to all appearance deserted, presumably owing to the disturbances of the previous day. The eggs were cold to the touch and covered with drops of water from a shower which had passed over earlier in the morning. Thus, on revisiting the nesting site on the 19th, with little hope of seeing the nest occupied, we were delighted to find that the greenshank had returned and was sitting closely. On the morning of the 20th we moved the tent closer to the nest, and again in the evening. The greenshank, on flying off, alighted on the top of a fir tree near, repeatedly uttering her wild cry. By May 23 the hide was moved to within fifteen feet of the nest. It was covered over with layers of fir branches and was so inconspicuous that it was difficult to see until one was almost upon it. On this day I entered the tent, being covered in afterwards by my companion, who walked on past the nest to distract the bird's attention. After calling loudly the greenshank walked silently up and settled unsuspecting on her eggs. Upon my imitating, or attempting to imitate, a curlew's whistle, she left the eggs instantly but quickly returned, nor would she move again even although the same whistling was repeated loudly and frequently. She seemed to think the noise came – as it should have done – from the sky, for on hearing it she looked skyward.

On May 26, a day of brilliant sunshine and tropical heat, the sitting greenshank was again visited and the hiding tent moved to about eight feet from the nest. After I had been closed up in the hide the greenshank quickly returned but this time she was wary, not liking the look of the lens which peered out at her through a hole cut in the front of the hide. At the end of ninety minutes she had not ventured on to her eggs. I decided that a further vigil would be necessary. Curiously enough on this second time the mother returned within five minutes to a point a foot or two from the eggs but lacked courage to settle down on them.

She brooded imaginary eggs in other places, but the eye of the camera staring at her was too much for her nerves. Not many minutes elapsed before her mate flew soothingly to her with soft and very musical flute-like calls. Then he walked past close to the eggs, apparently in the endeavour to discover the cause of his mate's alarm. Calling softly to her he took wing, whereupon she joined him, and they both flew across to the lochside to feed. The hen returned after about fifteen minutes but instead of brooding her eggs – knowing, no doubt, that in the warm sunshine they would come to no harm – stood motionless near the nest, dozing.

At last she did brood the eggs for a few minutes, panting continuously in the great heat. The cock during this time flew up into the air with quick wing beats uttering flute-like calls very much after the manner of the redshank during its nesting season but the notes were deeper and more musical than those of the latter bird. Two of the eggs were just commencing to chip.

On May 29 the eggs were still unhatched but one of the chicks could be heard hammering on the shell. The greenshank was now comparatively indifferent to the hide, returning almost at once to the nest and, after calling repeatedly with short, sharp whistling cries, walking confidently on to her eggs. On the afternoon of May 30 we found, on visiting the nest, that the small greenshanks had hatched out. I entered the hide at 3.30 p.m. and remained till 5.05 p.m. The mother greenshank seemed very proud of her young family, brooding them contentedly and pecking occasionally at a piece of broken eggshell lying just outside the nest. At 4.50 p.m. she suddenly sprang up on the nest, then flew off calling. She soon returned however. One of the chicks was restless and would not remain beneath her. On these occasions she would push it gently under her breast with her bill.

Early on the morning of May 31 we visited the nest for the last time. The chicks were still beside the nest but about 9 a.m. the mother greenshank led her young brood to a rush-fringed pool for their first feed. Here we left them, wishing them well and hoping that they would be successful in avoiding the many dangers that beset the chicks of ground nesting birds.

WON-21

THE PARASITIC CUCKOO

The meadow pipit is victimised more than any bird by the cuckoo, probably because they are often plentiful on the moors where there are few other birds for the marauder to victimise. The cuckoo does not invariably lay her egg actually in the nest of the victim, and in one instance a meadow pipit's nest was found under a rock in such a position that a cuckoo could not possibly have entered the hollow but must have deposited the egg outside and then placed it in the nest by means of her bill. Probably this is more often the case than is generally supposed – cuckoos have been shot while carrying eggs. An extraordinary thing, when the size of the bird is taken into consideration, is the smallness of the cuckoo's egg. When laid in a meadow pipit's nest it can scarcely be distinguished from the eggs of the rightful owner, so alike are they in size and markings. The meadow pipit is an interesting bird. It's call-note is an oft-repeated 'zizick, zizick' or 'sphink, sphink' while the male has a song very like his near relative, the tree pipit. Flying to a good height, he descends precipitately to the ground, uttering his song the while, but the notes he uses on his ascent are different from those uttered during the downward flight. The first brood are able to look after themselves by the month of June when the majority of the parent birds start housekeeping afresh and I have seen newly hatched young as late as the middle of July. They are very anxious when any danger threatens their young and fly restlessly around the intruder with their bills full of food, calling incessantly. (Having food in their mouths in no way interferes with their call-notes). The birds feed their young principally on insects, daddy-long-legs being a favourite morsel. Even as late as August an occasional meadow pipit will be seen collecting food for her brood but by this month the majority of the birds have finished their nesting cares. Until late October or even November they linger at the nesting haunts as if they would, were there a sufficient supply of food, prefer to remain on the uplands.

COH-12

GROUSE NOTES

A friend walking across a moor one day in May discovered a curious nest. A widgeon and grouse were laying together and an equal number of eggs of both birds were present. Unfortunately the nest was robbed or deserted before it could be seen whether the grouse or the widgeon took on the job of hatching the eggs. Not so many years ago widgeon and scoter nested only in the most northerly counties of Scotland. Since then, the widgeon has spread south and now nests in most parts of Scotland but the scoter remains a northern species and is seen by few.

Another interesting record is that of a grouse and a grey hen [female blackcock] laying in the same nest. When first the nest was found the grouse was in charge. There were thirteen eggs, six grouse and seven grey hen. My friend visited the nest the following morning and noticed that the grey hen was taking her turn on the eggs and twice subsequently he saw the red grouse patiently awaiting the grey hen's departure. The grouse's period of incubation is some days shorter than the grey hen's and so the grouse's eggs hatched out before those of the grey hen began to chip. Apparently the red grouse was in charge of the nest at the time of hatching as she was seen with her six sturdy chicks. The grey hen did not return to hatch out her own eggs. Perhaps she was disgusted by the untidy eggshells in the nest.

ITH-31

Early one April morning I crossed by car from Aviemore to Inverness. At Aviemore the air was heavy and the mist was low on the hills. Before I arrived at Slochd summit, where the road is 1,300 feet above sea level, I had entered clouds and the cloud canopy remained with me until I had almost reached Inverness. The mist had an interesting effect on bird life. At the roadside a hen grouse was feeding. She did not attempt to fly as my car neared her but just as the motor was on her she flew deliberately across in front, and although I was travelling slowly the radiator struck her a glancing blow. Lest I shall be accused of furious driving may I say that my motor-car is now in its twenty-third year and I feel proud when I travel twenty miles an hour. Had I been driving a faster car the grouse would undoubtedly have been killed, as it was she lay on the road apparently badly inured. My wife walked back to pick her up but the grouse was evidently merely stunned for she rose without difficulty and flew strongly up the hillside. When she reached the heather she was quickly joined by her anxious mate who had been a spectator of the accident from his perch on a small rock.

ITH-31

In this forest glen I saw a tragedy so swift and strange as to be almost unbelievable. A pair of grouse rose from opposite banks of the stream where they had been sunning themselves. The cock grouse few, crowing, up the burn and the hen followed him, still above the opposite bank. On her course was a small isolated rock. She must have been looking sideways toward her mate and flying blind for she charged the rock in full flight, rebounded two yards and lay lifeless on the heather.

AWP-37

THE OSPREY STORY

The osprey's last nesting place in this area was the ruined castle on Loch an Eilein, a beautiful loch in Rothiemurchus Forest. The last year in which the ospreys there reared young was in 1897. In 1899 two ospreys arrived on April 3 and subsequently nested. A third osprey then appeared on the scene. Much fighting followed, during which the eggs were broken and fell from the ruined tower into the loch. This was apparently the last year in which eggs were laid at Loch an Eilein. C.G. Cash, in Vols. IV and V of the *Cairngorm Club Journal*, gives a contemporary account of the nesting of the birds, states that two ospreys arrived at Loch an Eilein in 1900 but did not nest; it was thought they nested in Glen Feshie as four birds later in the year were seen there. In 1901 a single osprey arrived and was seen fighting above Ord Ban with a golden eagle. A single bird came in 1902 for the last time. In his article C.G. Cash mentions that he used to swim in Loch an Eilein before breakfast and the osprey at first alarmed him by flying above him as he swam and uttering its screaming cry. This writer mentions that in the years 1842–48 a pair of ospreys nested on the ruins of the old lodge at Loch Morlich. He quotes Lewis Dunbar as saying that these ospreys moved their young to another place if they were disturbed. I have more than once heard of the golden eagle doing this.

The Grants of Rothiemurchus, on whose territory the Loch an Eilein ospreys nested, did what they could to protect the birds during the nesting season and in 1893 John Peter Grant of Rothiemurchus and Donald Cameron of Lochiel were each awarded a silver medal by the Zoological Society of London, 'in recognition of the efforts made to protect the osprey in their respective districts.'

Shortly before the ospreys finally disappeared from the district a second eyrie was found in a tree on the shore of Loch Morlich but, not being on an island, this nest could not be protected. Indeed the nest on Loch an Eilein was sometimes robbed, although the boat on the loch was padlocked during the nesting season of the birds.

The almost legendary daring of one egg collector, who swam over to the island during a spell of Arctic April weather when six inches of snow covered the ground, used to be spoken of by the old people of the district. On a night of this kind there was apparently no watch on the shore of the loch and the would-be despoiler swam naked across the loch in the darkness, scaled the ruins of the castle and reached the nest. Here he suddenly realised that he had left his cap behind on the mainland shore – the cap which, firmly on his head, was to hold the precious eggs during the return swim. On the outward swim he had towed a rope, held by a companion on the shore, lest he should be overcome by cramp and he now found the rope to be of service for, taking an egg in either hand and lying on his back, he was drawn back to the shore. Half-way across he was seized with cramp but was pulled safely ashore. One would have thought that a single experience of this kind would have been sufficient for any man but the same nest robber in a subsequent season swam out to the island under cover of darkness and again robbed the nest. On this occasion he almost succeeded in capturing the owner of the nest; the osprey realising the danger only when his hand actually touched her.

The Highland ospreys had enemies not only at their summer haunts, they were shot in the south of England during their migration, and Highland landowners like Grant and Cameron who did their utmost to protect their ospreys fought a losing battle. There are rumours from time to time that a pair of ospreys have reared their young on some unfrequented Scottish loch but I am doubtful of these reports, although I realise that close secrecy is of the greatest importance if a wandering pair of ospreys should ever nest in the Highlands.

There is, for the time being at all events, a lessening of the activities of egg collectors and eagles have not done badly in recent years in the Cairngorm area. Unfortunately they are most conservative birds and return year after year to the same eyrie, or to one of two eyries, which in time become known. Were they to change their nesting site yearly like most birds they would be hard to locate in the old pine forest. It is surprising how difficult it is to find an eagle's eyrie in a tree.

HOS-51

Quite a number of ospreys were killed in Britain during the summer of 1930 and it would seem the ospreys of Scandinavia (whence come most of our wanderers) are on the increase. It is a thousand pities that this grand bird should be shot on sight when it appears in Britain. One of these ospreys was seen at the roadside at Grantown on Spey by a carter who killed the bird with a blow to the head. He did not perhaps know that he was destroying one of our rarest British birds. The osprey had a fractured wing, and was so thin that it could not have tasted food for days. Grantown is not far from Loch an Eilein where the osprey nested for generations. On Loch Arkaig, in western Inverness-shire, the osprey nested until 1908. On another loch in Inverness-shire a pair of ospreys nested and reared two young in 1910. Their eyrie was known to very few people and although the tree in which it was placed was in sight of a road I am informed that it was never discovered by a stranger. I have seen that old tree, a small Scots fir which can be climbed with ease. There is no sign of the eyrie on the tree now. Not far from the osprey's haunt a curlew with depraved tastes lived and was shot by a keeper as it was swallowing a new-hatched meadow pipit!

ITH-31

The return of the ospreys to nest successfully on a Scots fir in Strathspey marked the beginning of a remarkable record of success by the Royal Society for the Protection of Birds in osprey protection. The osprey, handsome, inoffensive, living entirely on fish, nested in Scotland a hundred years ago. It was shot and the eggs were taken in the days long before bird conservation was thought of and by the early years of the present century had been wiped out as a nesting species. The species continued to nest successfully in Sweden and Finland and it is possible that a pair from that area when they passed over Strathspey on their northward migration in spring, seeing an area that resembled their homeland, decided to nest here. They built an eyrie, indeed several eyries, but their eggs were taken.

Then in 1958 the Royal Society for the Protection of Birds began Operation Osprey. The first year despite a careful watch the eggs were taken on an exceptionally dark and misty night but since then a remarkable series of successful seasons still continue as I write in the autumn of 1970. During the twelve seasons beginning in 1959, a twenty-four-hour watch has been mounted immediately the ospreys arrive (the male usually arrives several days before the female). The only unsuccessful years were 1963 and 1966 – in each of these the nest and eggs were destroyed by a gale. In each of the other seasons young have been successfully hatched and reared. For this happy result George Waterston, the Scottish Representative of the Society and a team of enthusiastic helpers deserved the thanks and admiration of all bird lovers.

The eyrie is on the crown of an old Scots fir growing on a small dry knoll in typical greenshank country where, on much of the spongy, acid ground, old trees scarcely the height of a man have a struggle to maintain life. The osprey's tree, growing on drier ground, is higher than most. During my first watch the young ospreys, hatched about ten days before, were still in down, chocolate-brown on the head and white on the back. The father of the family brought all the food; the mother never fished and was almost continuously at the nest. The prey consisted, without exception, of fish. One large sea-tout was brought in, but most of the fish were brown trout weighing from about ½ lb to 1½ lbs.

Three weeks later, when I again saw the eyrie the young were full-feathered and had even grown the characteristic crest. On 26th July, excited by a strong wind from the south-east, the most forward of the young birds was flapping its wings vigorously and jumping from the eyrie almost a foot into the air. I could see the pale edgings to the feathers of the neck and mantle, absent in the parent birds, otherwise there was little to distinguish young from adults.

The female osprey left the nest during my watch, sailed overhead and then, in full flight, broke off a branch from a lifeless, bleached fir, carried it back and carefully built it into the eyrie. All the branches, brought by cock or hen, were broken off in flight and their sharp crack could be heard. The female watched intently as a pair of swifts approached the nest against the wind. The male appeared, carrying a fish whose amber fins glistened in the sun. He laid it in the eyrie, then flew to his usual perch on a neighbouring dead tree.

Later that evening I returned to the osprey hide. Herring gulls were slanting in from the east. The high tops of the Cairngorms were hidden in cloud. At 8.20 the male osprey set out on his evening fishing expedition, his flight westward as usual rather low above the dark pines. Midges had eagerly invaded the hide before I left in gathering rain.

Three days later, prolonged rain was ending as I approached the osprey country. The air was calm, and each pine needle glistened as its pendulous raindrop caught the light. The effect on the forest was as if a light snow shower had fallen. At noon the male osprey left his dead and whitened tree and set out for the invisible Spey. He had previously flown in twice, at very short intervals, each time with moss in one foot. The female had perched, high and prominent on the eyrie's edge, preening; in the same position stood her largest nestling.

The male returned with a fish at one o'clock. The strong light shone on his crest and white breast, mottled with brown, as he prepared to alight. There was then much activity in the eyrie, the female osprey feeding the young and both male and female carrying in pine branches, some of considerable size. How different the golden eagle's behaviour at this stage: the male eagle would arrive with prey and, having left it in the nest, would almost at once have taken wing, leaving the eaglet to pluck and eat as best it could.

Later, after chasing off a carrion crow, the female osprey continued to repair the eyrie, perhaps because it had suffered from the prolonged rain. The young ospreys were doing most vigorous and excited wing exercises, one of them for a moment becoming completely airborne and rising perhaps a couple of feet in the air. It held on, during its wing-flapping, to small pine branches loose in the eyrie, apparently to act as ballast. The mother brought from the moor a very large ball of moss. When she placed it on the floor of the eyrie she had difficulty in freeing her claws of it.

At four o'clock I saw, for little more than a second, the male pass a dead pine some distance away, carrying a fat trout of perhaps a pound in weight. When he disappeared from view, I expected him to arrive within a minute at the eyrie but had to wait three-quarters of an hour before he came. He had evidently been in the female's view, for she had often called. In the interval the male had clearly been feeding on the trout for when he brought it in, there was scarcely more than half the fish left, the head and shoulder had been eaten. The female picked up the trout, carried it to a dead tree, and daintily fed on it.

After five minutes she climbed into the air a considerable distance then flew in with the trout and at once offered small morsels to the smallest chick. Big brother meanwhile indulged in strenuous wing exercises with tail held fan-shaped. He faced the chilly north-east breeze and the low clouds, which brought a sharp and sudden shower, through which a wandering roe deer barked hoarsely.

My last morning (30th July) in the hide was calm and grey. The strongest of the three young ospreys watched with interest a swift and, later, seagulls flying high overhead. He then began his usual wing exercises and lifted a few inches above the floor of the eyrie a small stick perhaps six inches long. Suddenly he rose almost vertically into the air and hovered over the eyrie in masterly fashion, keeping station perhaps six feet above the floor of the nest. The remarkable thing was that he carried out this operation perfectly, as a helicopter might have done; with less skill and precision he might easily have flown beyond the eyrie, on to which he made an easy landing. The first hover-flight of a young osprey was a thrilling sight. I doubt whether the young of any other species rise vertically from the nest and return thus to it on a first flight.

A little later the father came in with a large dead branch held in one foot. Male and female flew off side by side. Flying thus, they gave a display, dropping and retracting legs and talons. An hour and a half later the male was seen with a large trout. As he stood on a dead tree, I could, through my glass, see him eating the shoulder of the fish. The trout was still alive, and occasionally flapped its tail feebly. The young ospreys would soon leave their sanctuary and face the dangers which beset all birds of prey.

HS-71

Seton Gordon would be amazed and delighted if he could come back today and see the technological wonders of watching ospreys at Loch Garten or Loch of the Lowes, the sea eagles on Mull or the gannets on the Bass Rock. The hopes he held for the future have indeed been rewarded.

An oystercatcher approaching its well-disguised nest

Blackcock at lek

The elusive greenshank at its nest

A greyhen (female blackcock) on its nest

Crested tit

A trio of merlin chicks in their heather-hidden nest

A male merlin brooding eggs laid in an old hoodie crow's nest in deep heather

Above: The young Seton Gordon at one of the remnant snowbeds he studied all his life

Right: Young kestrels

Above: A later picture (c.1920) looking into the Garbh Choire snowbed

Left: Summer cornices lingering on Braeriach

Seton Gordon's picture of 'the home of the water Ouzel' (Dipper)

The gentle touch of winter

Above: Red deer calf

Left: Boulders washed down in a Cairngorms spate

The River Avon below Inchrory

Falls of Corriemulzie, taken in 1910

The River Dee at Invercauld

The 'chalet' at Aboyne from which Seton Gordon set forth on early explorations

Seton Gordon in his car in 1906

Seton Gordon, third from right judging piping at a Braemar gathering

A youthful Seton Gordon with one of the old keepers he so admired and learned from

Above: The end of a day's stalking on the height

Left: Deerstalker Bob Scott at the Derry

Searching for Cairngorm stones

Coire Bhrochain, Braeriach, where Cairngorms were once found

Stags grazing in Glen Feshie

Stags in velvet

Above: Red deer calf

Left: A Cairngorm stream in winter

8

Eternal Snows?

One topic Seton Gordon returned to many times over the years was the possibility of Scotland having a corner where the snow never disappeared. The topic appears in his second book The Charm of the Hills, *1912, but mentions facts from earlier years so he must have started his studies while still in his teens. He reported regularly on the topic in the years prior to the First World War. The first passage came from this early book, the next from* Highland Year, *1944 and the final passage from his last book* Highland Summer, *1971.*

THE ETERNAL SNOWS OF THE CAIRNGORMS

Many assert that Lochnagar has the distinction of carrying perpetual snows in its corries but I have never been able to confirm this and if by any chance an eternal snowfield does linger on this mountain it is in a most unfrequented spot. Beinn a' Bhuird (3,918 feet) is probably the farthest east of the Cairngorms to have a snowy corrie of interest as a few hundred feet below the stony plateau is a snow-wreath which often remains on the hill-side throughout the year. In 1907 this was the case and in 1908 it was not until the first days of October that the drift entirely disappeared. In 1909 the snow, though a small patch by October, never completely vanished and in July of 1910 was larger than usual. Heavy gales toward the end of August and many hours of continuous sunshine in September however caused it to disappear rapidly; it vanished between September 15 and 16.

When on the summit of Lochnagar on October 11, 1910, I had the exceptional experience of having under observation the whole of the Cairngorm range as visible from this point without being able to distinguish the least trace of snow. A few days spent on the Cairngorms at a slightly later date showed, however, that a considerable amount of old snow remained and I was fortunate in obtaining photographs of these snow-wreaths. A visit was paid one fine morning to a field that has never been known completely to disappear, even during the hottest summer. Lying at the extreme end of the Garbhchoire, in a corrie known as the Fuar Garbhchoire, *the cold, rough corrie*, it is sheltered from the mild winds from the south and west and, after mid-day, is in deep shadow. Readings taken with the aneroid show the height to be 3,600 feet and in this unfrequented corrie snow is always to be found. Even at the end of July the whole corrie was deep in snow but by the time of my visit it had dwindled until only four isolated patches remained. The largest was some 45 yards in length by 30 inches breadth and from 8 to 10 feet in depth. The middle field was, roughly, 30 yards in length and on either side were two small fields. Taken as a whole, the snowfields were wonderfully similar in extent to what they were at the corresponding season of 1909 though on July 17 of the present year there was more than twice as much snow in the corrie.

After visiting the snow-wreaths at the head of the Garbhchoire I crossed the desolate plateau of Braeriach, disturbing a golden eagle on the way, and looked over into the grand corrie of Loch Coire an Lochan, the highest loch in Great Britain. From the eastern side of the corrie I imagined I could make out a small field of dirty snow on the western slope but as the whole hillside had a sprinkling of fresh snow it was difficult to distinguish old from new. At the summit cairn of Braeriach I had been standing scanning Ben Nevis through the glasses in brilliant sunlight when suddenly a thick mist enveloped the hilltop where I was. The cloud came from the north-east and, on the sun shining through the mist, a curious horseshoe-shaped rainbow or glory appeared almost at my feet, and remained until the mist cleared off.

Another interesting expedition was made to Ben Muich Dhui which in its numerous corries can boast of a couple of snowfields which rarely, if ever, completely disappear. The first one visited was in the so-called Snowy Corrie, only a few hundred yards from the summit and almost 4,000 feet. I remember some years ago crossing the field towards the end of the September and finding it quite 300 yards in length but on this occasion the drift was only 60 yards in length by 30 inches breadth, and a couple of feet in depth. Following the Garbh Uisge I passed two more fields lying in sheltered hollows and a small drift still remained on the shores of a lochan just above Loch Etchachan. During the previous winter the heaviest storms came from a westerly direction and this fact accounted for snow lying at such a low level on Ben Muich Dhui after a summer on the hills of considerable warmth. The snow examined was ridged and furrowed in the most curious manner and presented much the same appearance as ripples on the surface of a loch. Near the margins it was more or less solid ice and all over was extremely hard. Probably owing to the fact that the snow is packed so firmly by winter gales it can resist the mild winds and long hours of sunshine during the summer months. I have known of a snowfield on the lower slopes of Ben Muich Dhui which, when measured in early April, was close on 100 feet in height and yet had completely disappeared by June 23. As regards the Snowy Corrie the snow is swirled for miles along the plateau in front of any north or north-westerly gale and is packed closely in the corrie.

From the highest snowfield on Ben Muich Dhui a stream of considerable size was issuing which, at first, seemed as though it must come from the melting snow but closer investigation showed that the burn issued from a spring farther up the hill-side and passed right through the drift. Here I found fresh traces of deer and roosting hollows of the ptarmigan. This grouse of the mountains seems to have an affection for snow and will roost on the surface of a lingering field even when the rest of the hill-side is clear. Another interesting expedition was paid to Ben Muich Dhui just before fresh snow fell, to the snowfields at the head of the Feith Bhuidhe burn which is the real source of the Avon. Here, lying on some giant slabs of rock, are several fields of snow which are usually found in the corrie even after the hottest summer. The day chosen for the expedition turned out one of the finest of the autumn. In Glen Derry I had a good view of a number of herds of deer, and in one case lay for close on half an hour watching a very fine stag driving off intruders from his following of hinds. He never allowed himself a moment's rest, either roaring or rushing here and there after numerous young stags which fled incontinently on his approach. Even his hinds had many uneasy moments when he was charging down upon them and moved off in a mildly protesting fashion.

On crossing the ridge to the north-west of Loch Etchachan, at a height of 3,900 feet, I had an excellent view of the snow and found that as many as five drifts were still remaining. On the way down to visit the lowest I had the good luck to watch a stoat running round among some rocks, quite unaware of my presence. A flock of ptarmigan rose quite near him and very beautiful they looked as they sped across the deep corrie of Loch Avon and reappeared in the sunlight on the slopes of Cairngorm. The three lowest snowfields were arranged in the form of a triangle at an approximate height of 3,500 feet and faced north-east. The one I visited was perhaps 50 yards across and some 10 to 12 feet in depth, its bed on rock and, like the field on Braeriach, was lying at a very steep angle – so much so that it was very difficult to obtain a footing on it. On the surface were fresh tracks of ptarmigan and mice. The temperature was considerably below the freezing point and a thin covering of fresh snow lay on the field but, in spite of this and the fact that icicles several inches thick covered the rocks, the snow was melting from beneath and the water as it dripped down was forming icicles.

After examining the three lower fields, I proceeded to a couple of large snow beds about a quarter of a mile to the south-west and facing almost due east. The largest of the drifts was found by the aneroid to be 3,700 feet and was by far the most extensive: 100 yards long by 60 broad. The depth must have been close on 14 feet and the remains of a cornice were still present. Another field alongside it was some 70 yards in length and at one point only a very thin snow bridge covered a burn running through the drift. The fact that in every case moss was found up to the extreme edge of the snow and that even when the latter was broken moss plants were found beneath its surface, seems to prove that in certain years the snow actually does disappear, though it says much for the hardiness of the moss that it can remain buried for so long without its vitality being impaired. Besides the snowfields mentioned, there is an extensive wreath on a north-eastern corrie between

Ben Muich Dhui and Cairngorm, which I was unable to investigate at close quarters though there was an excellent view of it from the high ground between Grantown-on-Spey and Tomintoul. The study of these snowfields is an intensely fascinating one and a series of observations taken at the fall of each year should in time produce interesting results.

COH-12

On one visit to the snowfields they were led astray by the lure of cairngorms, the semi-precious crystals which today are very seldom discovered. (See also 'Cairngorm Stones' at the end of Chapter 13; page 169.)

AN INTERRUPTION

Close by the drift we found fields of delicate parsley fern (which we have almost always found growing in proximity to snow) and the grass, not long freed from it snowy covering, was fresh and green. The snow-field, originally covering the whole of the corrie, had dwindled until it had split into four patches.

While measuring the drifts we noticed a vein of quartz running up the rock immediately above the snow and on examining it were delighted to see, embedded in the rocks, the points of some very fine cairngorms. The cairngorm is readily recognised by its hexagonal shape and tip pointed much after the manner of a sharpened pencil. The deeper the colour the more valuable the stone and on the present occasion the cairngorms were sherry coloured and good quality. The finest stones are often found embedded in a certain kind of clay, near a quartz vein, but lying quite free of the rock and as the clay was present in this instance, protruding from under a large rock, we determined to move the stone to see whether any cairngorms were actually beneath it.

Although the boulder seemed in an unstable position it took a couple of hours' hard work before it was dislodged and sent roaring down into the snow beneath. (One of the party was in a precarious position toward the end of the levering operations and it was feared that he would accompany the rock on its downward journey!) Sure enough, in the exposed clay numbers of cairngorms were found, of various sizes and shapes but not a few of them were perfectly formed, with scarcely a flaw. A thorough search was made – a search which was somewhat rudely interrupted by a boulder becoming dislodged from the top of the rocks perhaps 300 feet above us.

COH-12

SHRUNKEN SNOWBEDS

In October the snowbeds of the high hills are at their lowest ebb. Whether there is perpetual snow on any Scottish hill is a question of doubt. There are two hills which I have never seen free of snow: Ben Nevis, the highest hill in Scotland, and Braeriach.

Both of these snowfields lie beneath cliffs where they are sheltered from prevailing winds from the south west. In early summer these fields are of great depth and the snow gradually melts until, at the coming of the new snow, it is as hard as ice. I have known new snow cover the old for the winter as early as mid-September but its coming is usually in the second week in October. That autumn (1942) it was later than usual and on the 22nd of the month, when a friend and I visited the Braeriach snowbed, there was no fresh snow, although I believe the snow did arrive two days later. The old snowbed on this occasion was considerably smaller than I had ever seen it but was in no danger of melting.

The plants which have their home near these snowbeds have a short growing period, indeed, when the snow is slow in melting or after an usually snowy winter, they may have no growing season at all but may be imprisoned beneath the snow throughout the year. Phanerogams – this is the higher, flowering plants – can stand one year's imprisonment, perhaps more, but Cryptogams such as lichen or mosses are able to survive a much longer period beneath the snow. At the edge of the Braeriach snowbed are mosses which are not snow free once in ten years and which, even in the most favourable season, have less than a month's growth (late September and October) when there is little warmth in the air and frost, sometimes severe, at night. For the first time in my experience I found that the snow, this autumn of 1942, had receded beyond the edge of all plant growth for the stones then exposed were devoid even of lichen and for this reason appeared unusually clean.

Nearer to the snow than it was possible for grass to exist, I found small plants of *Saxifraga stellaris*, the comparatively long-stemmed white-flowered saxifrage, which grows freely on damp ground in the high corries of most Highland hills. But in this lonely, sunless corrie of Braeriach at a height of 3,600 feet there was no time for flowers to be formed, only the smallest of buds. A little farther from the snow, but still where grass could scarcely live, was a carpet of *Gnaphalium supinum* [now *Omalotheca supina*, the dwarf cudweed]. Then came the grass and, still farther away from the snow, the heather. The flower heads of the grass had been killed and whitened by an early frost before they had time to mature. Here one was sheltered from the westerly gale which rushed across the cliffs and poured the mist into the corrie in grey columns like aerial waterfalls.

HY-44

PERPETUAL SNOW?

"Is there perpetual snow in Scotland?" is a question often asked. There are snowbeds on several Scottish hills which remain unmelted through most summers. On one of the rare summer days when the shade temperature in Fort William stands at 80 degrees Fahrenheit the great snow-bed in the north-east corrie of Ben Nevis can still be seen from the main road near Inverlochy Castle. There is indeed a local saying, 'Lochiel will hold his lands so long as there is snow on the Ben'. The Macintyres of Glen Nodha [Noe] paid their rent, on Midsummer's Day of a 'white-fatted calf and a bucket of snow' taken from a high corrie of Cruachan Beannn above Loch Etive. The Munros of Foulis for centuries have held their lands on condition that they 'supplied a bucket of snow at the Palace of Holyroodhouse on Midsummer Day to cool the King's wine'. The Munros of Foulis were able to supply this snow because of Ben Wyvis, which rises near their ancestral home, where snow sometimes lies throughout the year. The Grants of Rothiemurchus, whose land on the Cairngorm Hills reaches a height of 2,248 feet have a tradition that they hold their land on condition that they supply the sovereign with a bucket of snow whenever asked.

The snowbed on Braeriach is almost within a stone's throw of the lands of Rothiemurchus but is just over the watershed in the deer forest of Mar, for long held by the MacDuffs. I have made observations on this snowfield for more than half a century and the only occasion I have seen it entirely disappear was in 1959. That summer in the Central Highlands was the warmest in living memory. In early September I made an expedition to the site of this snow which lies in one of the most remote areas of the Cairngorm Hills, near the boundary or 'march' between three great deer forests, Rothiemurchus, Mar and Glen Feshie.

It was a strange experience to be on the high hills in late summer with no lessening of the heat. The sky was cloudless; the heather bloom even at 2,500 feet above the sea was completely over and almost lifeless from the drought. The exceptional character of the season was shown by the second flowering of Alpine plants. At 2,500 feet above the sea there were red buds and pink flowers on *Azalea procumbens* and at 3,500 feet a plant of *Silene acaulis* carried a flower, perfectly formed. In the spray of the burns were golden blooms of the mountain species of the marsh marigold which I had never before seen flower in September. It was strange also to find that the water of these hill streams, usually ice-cold, was comparatively warm.

The Braeriach snow-bed lies at the west face of the wild, deep Garbh Choire, *the Rough Corrie*, approximately 3,600 feet above the sea and immediately below a sheer precipice 200 feet high which falls from the summit plateau. The snow is drifted to a great depth during the winter months. In late summer it becomes almost solid ice and it has been suggested that this may be the site of the last British glacier. In autumn the snow splits into several pockets which become discoloured by fine gravel and peat dust and might escape notice from the Lairig Ghru Pass, one of the few places from which this snow is visible. When I was on the pass this September morning I was surprised to see there was no snow visible. In order to make doubly sure, Morag the cairn terrier (she felt the unusual heat even more that I did) and I set out on the long and latterly steep climb over unstable boulders and screes to the site of the snow, the sun beating down with tropical heat.

As we approached our destination I realized how exceptional the conditions were that year. In the screes the attractive parsley fern had grown fresh young leaves and the hill grass was green as in early summer, the starry saxifrage was flowering a second time, and the seed of the cudweed in places formed a white carpet. At length we had climbed to the base of the precipice and stood where the snow should have been lying. It had gone, completely and without trace and, more remarkable, had disappeared two months before it could have been reinforced by the arrival of the first autumn snow. Gone were the small streams from the snow which usually moisten the ground beneath. Instead of being soft and damp, it was dry and even dusty.

Where, certainly for twenty-five years, the snow had remained, summer and winter, the rocks themselves were clean and bright as though newly quarried. By early afternoon the fierce sun was hidden by the precipice above and the air was cool.

The absence of bird life, throughout that long day's walk of fourteen hours, was remarkable. I did not see one ptarmigan or one grouse, never a soaring eagle cheered me nor a white-winged snow-bunting. The one bird I did see was a meadow pipit.

At half past six that evening, when I crossed the young Dee a short distance above its junction with the stream known as Allt Garbhchoire, the sun was setting behind the precipice of Braeriach above the site of the snow-bed I had visited. As the upper rim of the sun disappeared, glowing and quivering, a shaft of light shot into the sky towards the stony slopes of Cairntoul. While I walked south by the clear River Dee the sun bathed the high inhospitable dome of Ben MacDhui (4,300 feet) in a delicate pink glow and the rocks on dark Carn a' Mhaim became burnished gold – a truly alpine scene. In the evening light the marks of a recent cloudburst high on the face of Coire Bhrochain of Braeriach became conspicuous. Low in the southern sky the young moon now contended with the sunset. The path became indistinct as I crossed the shoulder of Carn a' Mhaim. A chill air drifted up from the river. The track was now almost invisible and progress slow. Of Morag there had for long been no sign. I realized how much the moon had meant to me as I now searched for my car which I had earlier left near the stalker's cottage at Luibeg fourteen hours earlier. The car at length loomed out of the blackness only a few feet from me and there, hopefully waiting, sat Morag.

That expedition was in the year 1959, and the snow certainly remained unmelted, summer and winter, for the next ten years [as he heard from Adam Watson who has continued this study to the present. Watson has recorded snow vanishing in the autumns of 1996, 2003 and 2006. (Information of 2009)].

HS-71

9

All Growing Things

Seton Gordon was always an all-round naturalist (the study of heathers for instance is an early piece by a young man who already had a vast store of knowledge) and many chapters in his books range over several topics whatever the main objective of that particular expedition. He just can't not share anything and everything with us. His love of the old Scots pine forest, indeed, for all tress, moor and mountains, shines forth in this chapter.

THE OLD FOREST

No British wood is more beautiful that the Old Caledonian Forest which extends eastward from dark Loch Arkaig in Lochiel's country to Strathspey and the upper waters of the Dee, and clothes the lower slopes of the Cairngorm Hills. These pine tress of Glen Mallie and Achnacarry, Glen Feshie and Mar, Rothiemurchus and Glen More, Abernethy and the King's Country of Ballochbuie, come of an ancient race. They are descended from trees which saw wolf and bear, wild boar and elk, roam through the heather in the open spaces of the forest. The oldest family of the land cannot trace its descent back so far as these sombre pines.

No tree has been planted in the Caledonian Forest; from father to son, throughout the centuries, the line is unbroken. The oldest of these pines today are perhaps three hundred years old. But let us in imagination see what the fathers and grandfathers of these old trees saw. Their day would have been when Bannockburn was fought, when the Wolf of Badenoch lived in his island fortress on Loch an Dorb, when the Lords of the Isles engaged in battle with the Kings of Scotland. And so, in the forest, a sense of the past, of far-off things, lingers still.

When the winter wind makes soft music in their topmost branches the trees tell of patience and quiet strength, they await the strengthening rays of the sun that will awaken them when spring comes again. Even at midwinter the old trees sleep lightly and when at noon the pale sun touches them their sap quickens and in their sleep they dream of approaching spring.

Scots pines are indeed the predominate trees but in some of the open spaces shapely junipers grow. The juniper is usually considered a bush or shrub but here it is a tree, sometimes only a little less in stature than the pines themselves and more graceful than they.

In late summer a red wave of heather blossom surges through the forest and sometimes in December the bloom in the shelter of the trees is still untouched by frost. The last of the red fruits of the cowberry are then hidden beneath their sheltering crown of leaves. In December the day is short, the forest is in darkness by four o'clock and, when the grey wind from the west herds the drifting clouds in low ragged companies across the slopes of the lesser hills and the snow-covered heights are hidden, dusk settles over the trees before sunset. How sombre the forest on those days! In the distance the trees appear black.

Perhaps as the forest lover walks by some old woodland track the sky clears overhead and a pathway of deep blue is seen though the clouds. Upon the shore of a forest loch small waves advance and eddies of wind ruffle and darken the water. The pine forest climbs the steep slopes where the golden eagle soars and the wild cat stalks the plump blackcock or the swaggering cock grouse upon his heathery knoll. The wind is soft, but snow-wreaths linger on these high forest slopes and in the shadowy light of a winter afternoon assume a tint of palest blue.

Perhaps the clouds lift and the upper slopes of the hill giants are seen, snowy slopes which in the twilight appear almost as dark as the clouds that drift across them. No trees may venture there. The land belongs to the clan of the ptarmigan who have lived on these hills from time immemorial and whose ancestry goes back as far as the old trees themselves. After deep prolonged snowfall when all food supply has failed them the ptarmigan descend to the forest. Once or twice only in a human generation, they may be seen flitting phantom-like through the old trees.

One midwinter day I recall. Along the valley of the Spey a frosty mist lay close and dense, as though a London fog had descended on the Highlands. But when I had gone a little way into the forest I saw ahead of me a flood of sunlight on the woodland path and in less than a minute I had left the mist behind and was walking through a fairy-like country. Overhead the sky was a deep glorious blue and no single cloud floated upon that wide arch. To the south the Cairngorm Hills rose, each deep corrie in shade, each western slope leaned to the life-giving rays of the sun. Near the crests of the hills deep shadow and sunshine met and the sudden transition from dark to light was inspiring. A soft primrose glow suffused the lower slopes. Not the faintest air stirred in the forest that day: the ground was white with rime, each birch tree a delicate tracery of frost-encrusted branches, each heather shoot encased in a frosty sheath. On a heathery knoll in a clearing grouse were calling, capercaillies were perched in the trees.

With silent flight the great birds dipped almost to the ground then swept out of view on wings that glinted in the low sun. Two mild-eyed hinds watched the disappearing capercaillies then themselves disappeared among the trees. At the edge of an open heathery space stood a pine immeasurably older than his fellows. Upon the bole, white with age, no bark remained and in the smooth trunk a woodpecker had bored out a symmetrical, round hole.

The sun dipped and the snowy slopes became a country of mystery. Slowly the mist curtain rose from the valley. Nearer and nearer it crept. Hiding the forest trees it wound sinuously along the course of a hill burn, drifting upward upon a damp chill air till at last it had reached the high ground and hid the silent peaks in ghostly embrace.

10W-33

THIS WORLD OF TREES

Scotland is proud of its ancient forests. The larch and spruce which now flourish in many Highland glens are beautiful but are foreigners far from their homelands. The Scots fir, *Pinus sylvestris*, was growing in Scottish glens from time immemorial. When I walk beneath the splendid firs of Ballochbuie and Mar; of Rothiemurchus, Glen Feshie and Rannoch, I realize that some of them were grown trees when the clans rose in support of Prince Charles in 1745. Ancestors of those grand trees flourished when Saint Columba crossed Scotland to preach the Christian faith to the Pictish King Brude at Inverness. Those were the days of the Druids – mighty men who had the power to change the direction of the wind, cover the land with a magic sea and call down lightning and tempest at their bidding.

Perhaps in the Forest of Mar the old firs are seen to best advantage. They have long been celebrated. In the year 1621 James VI wrote to the Earl of Mar asking him to send seed from the Scots firs of Mar for his new kingdom, England. At the same time he requested information on the type of ground most suited for the seed beds and for the planting of the young firs. Could it be possible that a few survive? I have little doubt that one of the oldest trees in Mar Forest, Craobh an Oir, *the Tree of Gold*, was already well grown in 1621. [See page 178 for the legend of this tree.]

Across the high tops towards the east is Glen Eanaich, a place-name Professor Watson, Celtic authority, believed came from the obsolete Gaelic Eanaich, meaning *Marsh*. In this glen stands another historic Scots fir, the Tree of the Return. For centuries the people of Rothiemurchus were accustomed to go, at the coming of summer, from their homes near the Spey to the summer shielings at the head of Glen Eanaich where, in the corrie above Loch Eanaich, the land is green and fertile. The stirks, and the cows with their sucking calves, were driven up Glen Eanaich a few days before the people themselves went to their summer homes. The drovers, when they had reached the old fir growing a little above the river flowing from the loch, left the beasts, and returned to Rothiemurchus. They knew the older beasts would remember the good grazing and would continue the journey by themselves to the head of the loch.

On July 8, 1923, the Tree of the Return narrowly escaped disaster. I was in the glen that day, on Braeriach above it, when perhaps the worst thunderstorm I have experienced broke overhead. That evening, when I returned through the glen, I saw that the flooded river had swept away heather, rocks and many trees on its mad rush. The Tree of the Return grows near an insignificant side-burn but the burn had deeply cut away the bank and had almost undermined the old fir. The last time I saw the Tree of the Return I realized that it was near the end of its life. [It has now gone.]

In the Caledonian Forest the Scots fir is the chief tree and it is sad that the forest is yearly decreasing. Great areas were felled during the Second World War. Even in the remote glens of Mar where there was no felling there is now no natural regeneration, not a seedling. The reason for this is that red deer eat each young tree as it appears above the heather. One might have thought that deer were always in the district but in olden times wolves roamed the forest of the Highlands and red deer were less numerous than they are at present. It is not too late to fence in considerable areas in order to allow the young firs to spring up in natural regeneration. If this is not done most of the glens of Mar Forest in a century or more will be as treeless as Glen Giusachan. Glen Giusachan is *Fir Tree Glen*, treeless now, yet one has only to traverse it to realize how appropriate the name must have been once. By the small, clear river are seen the roots and stumps of an ancient forest of Scots firs. Many of the stumps remain upright where the trees grew, others have been carried down the river in times of flood and lie, bleached, on the shingle banks. At one place where the Giusachan River has eaten into a high bank of peat the entire trunk of an old Scots fir is exposed after being buried for at least a thousand years. In Glen Giusachan the tree-line seems to have reached a height of 2,300 feet, in Glen Luibeg I have found it 2,400 feet. The limit in Mar and Rothiemurchus is approximately 2,000 feet. The only place, so far as I am aware, where this altitude is exceeded is in Rothiemurchus Forest above Loch Gamhna, on the slope which leads to Clach MhicCailein, *Argyll's Stone* where a few stunted firs grow just above the 2,000 feet level.

It is often said that the Scots fir is at its best in the Central Highlands because of the comparatively light rainfall there, but one has only to see the magnificent Scots firs near Loch Arkaig in Lochaber to realize that rainfall has little effect on this tree. (The annual rainfall there is about one hundred inches.) There are no finer Scots firs. West of Loch Arkaig, at Barrisdale where the rainfall is heavier still the Scots fir also flourishes. In Glen Etive, where the rainfall is sometimes as high as one hundred and sixty inches, old Scots firs may be seen on the upper reaches of the glen. We of this generation must see that Scotland's tree in its natural native state is not ruth-lessly felled and we should do our best to ensure that conditions are favourable for the old firs to regenerate naturally.

HD-63

BIRCH AND ASPEN

After a cold and backward spring, birches are sometimes late in uncurling their scented leaves. Among cold springs the coldest and latest I remember was 1923. I was at Aviemore during the last week of May, leaving on the morning of the 29th. As the train pulled out of the station I well remember looking at the weeping birches that clothe the face of Craigellachie: the whole wood was of the red-brown tint associated with February and March with not the faintest tinge of green to be seen and June only three days off. Late budding gives the birch a short flowering season and it is not uncommon for the trees to be caught by an autumn frost while yet in the full vigour of their growth. Just as fields of oats in the upper straths of Dee, Don and Spey are sometimes caught and shrivelled while the ears are still green and far from ripe so are the leaves of the birch sharply warned that their time here is short. But birch leaves are of a tougher fibre than the heads of grain and it needs several nights of frost to turn them from green to gold. The colour of the birch in its autumn glory is seen at its best against the dark background of pines. The entrance to the Lairig Ghru pass is one of the best places I know for this. Birches are scarce and that is to their advantage when a single golden birch stands out in glory amid the dark firs – and may be seen at a distance of several miles.

The aspen is a later budder than the birch and is the latest tree, with the possible exception of the ash, to come into leaf in the Highlands. But the leaves of the aspen are more delicate than those of the birch and, although the aspen is still bare in spring when the birch is in leaf, it is gaunt and leafless once more in autumn when the birch is still in the beauty of its foliage. Aspen leaves cease to tremble in autumn shortly before they fall.

During a sombre day in the autumn of 1942 I happened to be walking with a friend in Rothiemurchus Forest and near the upper fringe of the pines, where they grew stunted and gnarled because of the fury of the hill winds, we passed a solitary aspen, large and well-formed (for it was in comparative shelter) and so bright were its golden leaves it seemed as though a mystic fire burned within that tree giving an added glory.

For some of us at times it is possible to see beyond the material form of a tree into what, for want of a better word, I will term its etheric and less gross being. One birch in particular I have in mind, a tree perhaps fifty years old, its stem, with almost pure white bark, straight and graceful, its branches pendulous and often shaken by the wind for it grows on a hillside without shelter. Sometimes I have looked long upon that tree and have seen it as it were dissolve in thought and assume a new and delicate beauty not of this world. Those who have seen as I have seen will understand me and what I am endeavouring to describe.

HY-44

OUR HEATHERS

During the months of late summer the plants of heather with their countless blossoms transform mile upon mile of lonely moorland from dark brown to pink and crimson – colours to delight the eye.

In the Highlands three species of heather are met with: the common ling, the typical heather of the grouse moors, *Calluna vulgaris*; the bell heather, *Erica cinerea*; and the more pinkish-flowered *Erica tetralix*, or cat heather, as it is sometimes called. [More commonly cross-leaved heath.]

Of the three, *Erica cinerea* is perhaps the first to blossom and is often a month ahead of the ling. It grows at its best in very dry situations and sometimes I have seen it flowering with wonderfully vivid blooms of crimson in the dried-up course of some hill stream where no soil was apparent. It frequently appears first after the burning of a moor, holds the field for a few years, and is then gradually mastered by *Calluna vulgaris*.

The bell heather has by far the most powerful scent of all the heathers; a July visit to a moor where this heather grows in profusion, when the air is still and the sun shines strongly, will live long in the memory by reason of the wonderful colouring of its blossoms (visible over many miles) and the fine scent which, from its freshness and purity, is a thing to delight the senses.

Erica tetralix may at once be recognized by the paler colour of its flowers. Unlike *E. cinerea*, it is fond of boggy ground, is rarely found on dry hillsides and the plants do not grow in such close proximity nor so densely as those of the other two species. *E. tetralix* continues to send out flower shoots throughout the summer whereas the bell heather and ling do so only exceptionally. This latter species, besides being the most common, is also found at the greatest elevations. In the Cairngorms the limit of the growth of ling is about 3,300 feet but it is not often seen above the 3,000 line. During the last 500 feet the plants show a creeping or prostrate habit and rarely, if ever, produces any flowers. I have frequently come across clumps of white heather at high levels.

The ling seems to be one of the slowest recoverers from the effects of winter snow. Snow drifted into a corrie by heavy winter gales may lie till late in the spring or well into summer and the ling, when first exposed, is found to be pressed flat on the ground. If conditions are favourable the plants gradually assume the upright position once more but should the weight of snow have been unusually great or the melting protracted, the heather remains prostrate, or partially so, throughout the season, though they endeavour to shoot in that position as far as the short period of warm weather permits them. Heather is rarely killed by drought, being an essentially *zerophytic* plant, so the small leaves are tightly rolled back at all times, protecting the *stomata* or breathing pores from hot sunshine or strong drying winds, and thus preventing too rapid transpiration.

But the remarkable drought which characterized the summer of 1919 was sufficient to kill outright large stretches of both *Calluna vulgaris* and *Erica cinerea*, the plants becoming absolutely dead. In other cases the flower buds failed to open and either remained dormant, blossoming long after their time, or dropped to the ground. The contrast during the last days of August, 1919 between the heather in central Aberdeenshire and the Hebrides was striking; in the latter summer had been uniformly wet and cold whereas in Aberdeenshire the drought was the most severe for half a century. White heather of the three species is not uncommonly met with. *Calluna vulgaris* gives the largest areas but owning to the craze for lucky white heather, these areas are rapidly decreasing in more accessible districts.

WON-21

DAMAGE AND RECOVERY

In the spring of 1930 the heather showed little signs of recovering from the intense frost of February 1929. Large areas of long heather which at the time of the frost were unprotected by a covering of snow were killed outright. Far up some lonely glen at the edge of the Old Caledonian pine forest one saw, here and there, a juniper tree of a uniform reddish-brown, as lifeless as the heather. That memorable frost was accompanied by a gale which dried up the life-juices of bush and tree more thoroughly than the most prolonged drought of summer. The ground was frozen as hard as iron and so the plants were unable to replace the moisture lost by evaporation. In the summer following the protective effects of snow were seen. On the high grounds where the heather had been covered with snow during the cold spell it was green and vigorous in June, on the lower grounds it was red and withered and the small leaves were dropping off.

In places the Scots firs were as red as though singed by fire but the deciduous tress did not suffer and in April the aspen in Highland glens hung out as usual their innumerable dark red catkins. The Gaels have an old legend that the aspen gave the wood for the cross of Christ and that is why its leaves tremble in sadness and shake throughout the long breathless summer days.

Each of the noble trees of Glen Feshie is self-sown. The fierce gale of January 1927 did great damage in this old pine forest. Trees that had stood through many generations were uprooted by the violence of that hurricane. Beside an old cottage a rowan shared their fate. The rowan (mountain ash) was in olden times planted near a dwelling to keep away the fairies. [Never mind olden times; I've done this always after flitting and I know others have too.]

ITH-31

CAIRNGORM BERRIES

Summer is gone. Already the high tops have received their second coating of autumn snow, and the birches and hill grasses show golden and brown against the dark hillsides. It is now that the berries of the hills are at their best. As yet they are untouched by the frosts, and the grouse and ptarmigan have not thinned their numbers so everywhere one may wander on the hills the berries delight the eye with their rich delicate colouring.

Perhaps the two best know are the blaeberry (bilberry in the south) *Vaccinium myritillus* and the cranberry (more properly cowberry) *Vaccinium vitis-idaea*. One frequently finds the two growing profusely together and their season of ripening is nearly the same. The blaeberry is one of the very few hill plants that is deciduous – that is, it sheds its leaves each autumn. There is no more delightful scent of the high hills than the aroma of countless blaeberry plants on a hot sunny day. The blaeberry, far more that the cranberry, is a true Alpine plant, and is found as high as between the 3,000-foot and 4,000-foot levels, though its fruit here is indifferent. [I've enjoyed delicious blaeberries as late as November upon the slopes of Braeriach overlooking the Pools of Dee.] The fruit of the blaeberry is of a dark blue colour, comparatively sweet to the taste and the only berry with which it is likely to be confused is the crowberry, *Empetrum nigrum*, but whereas the leaves of the blaeberry are deciduous and delicate, those of the crowberry are heath-like and sturdy.

The cranberry – for it is always thus that the cowberry is named in Scotland – is a plant of the lower hills and pine forests rather than the high tops. In height it is considerably less than the blaeberry and it retains its sturdy leaves throughout winter. The flowers are borne in a cluster at the apex of the stem, usually white, but may sometimes be found of varying shades of pink. Almost alone amongst hill plants the cranberry may be found flowering during every month of summer and even in late autumn when there is little or no chance of the berries coming to maturity. The fruit of the cranberry is of dark red and one flower stem often bears quite a number of the berries, but the stem is sturdy and is quite able to carry the weight of the fruit.

The leaves of both blaeberry and cranberry frequently turn to flaming red at the approach of autumn. I noticed in Rothiemurchus during a recent summer that shortly after producing their leaves the blaeberry plants were almost everywhere attacked by a species of caterpillar and their leaves rolled up into unsightly withered balls. The disastrous fire which swept Rothiemurchus Forest in June 1920, was largely aided by this fact for the thick undergrowth of blaeberry plants, instead of offering a moist barrier to the flames, was almost as dry and inflammable as the heather itself.

A plant closely akin to the cranberry in its fruit is the bearberry, *Arctostaphylos uva-ursi*. Its berries are somewhat smaller than those of the former plant and of a slightly lighter red. The habit and appearance of the two plants are however entirely different for the cranberry grows erect and sturdy while the bearberry creeps prostrate over the hills. Although the two species may be found growing together, the bearberry is the more Alpine and is usually met with on the high ground, 3,000 feet and over. Owing to this fact its habit is prostrate, the better to withstand the gales which frequently sweep the high hills. The bearberry fruits late and its berries are frequently buried, while still at their best, beneath the first winter snowfall. I have noticed frequently while on the high hills in winter with only a few inches of snow on the ground that at almost every step I crushed some bearberries underfoot, their juice appearing through the snow and staining it red.

A plant little known on the hills is the great bilberry *Vaccinium uliginosum*. The stems, unlike those of the blaeberry, are stout and woody and the leaves are more glaucous in colour. The great bilberry does not seem to be found so near the sea level as the common nor does it reach such great heights. Its berries too are smaller and more bitter. I have only exceptionally seen it bearing fruit on the Cairngorm Hills.

Perhaps of all the hill berries the crowberry, *Empetrum nigrum*, is the most alpine. It is extremely hardy and seems impervious to cold winds and frosts. The leaves are small and of a dark colour and are very *zerophytic* (drought-withstanding). The flower is barely noticeable but the berries are of almost similar size to those of the blaeberry, only black and sour. The shoots of the crowberry are eaten in winter by the ptarmigan and probably the berries also.

The true cranberry, as distinct from the cowberry which, curiously enough, everywhere in Scotland usurps its name, is known to scientists as *V. oxycoccus*. It is comparatively rare, prostrate, resembling the bearberry rather than *V. vitis-idaea*.

Its berries are more transparent and inclined to yellow rather than red and it grows mainly on boggy ground.

A plant widely different from any of those mentioned above is the cloudberry or avern (sometimes avron) *Rubus chamaemorus*. It is in its habits comparatively local but is usually found on or near boggy ground. I have seen it on the Cairngorms well over 3,000 feet up but here it is late in forming its flowers and the fruits rarely mature. A delicate plant, it withers quickly when plucked and the fragile white blossom has a short life. The fruit before ripening is of a reddish colour which, curiously enough, turns more to yellow – not a darker red – as the berry becomes mature. When the plants grow in sufficient profusion, as in the Borders, the berries are gathered and make excellent jam.

WON-21

FLOWERS SET FREE

With the passing of the years I am inclined to leave a flower on its stalk although I often stoop down to breathe in the fragrance of a wild rose or a scented orchis, or the honey scent of a clustered head of the rosy moss campion opening its hardy flowers close to the blinding glare from some snowfield of the high Cairngorms. The most exquisite pictures of flowers stored in my mind are the blossoms that grew, free as the air they breathed, and not gathered into a vase within the confines of a room. In his poem *Forbearance*, Ralph Waldo Emerson puts things very well:

> *Hast thou named all the birds without a gun?*
> *Loved the wood-rose, and left it on its stalk?*
> *At rich men's tables eaten bread and pulse?*
> *Unarmed, faced danger with a heart of trust?*
> *And loved so well a high behaviour,*
> *In man or maid, that thou from speech refrained,*
> *Nobility more nobly to repay?*
> *O, be my friend, and teach me to be thine!*

Emerson in one of the essays recalls that the ancients called beauty the flowering of virtue. But was he right when he wrote: 'Flowers so strictly belong to youth, that we adult men soon come to feel that their beautiful generations concern us not, we have had our day, now let the children have theirs. The flowers jilt us, and we are old bachelors with their ridiculous tenderness.'?

With some of us at least our love of flowers continues unchanged, and even intensified, with the passing years, the beauty of a flower, a bird, a cloud, sunset and sunrise, evoke in us the same response in later, more anxious years, as in the fullness of youth.

HY-44

10

Deeside Approaches

The ascents of Deeside's Morven and Mount Keen appeared in one of his earliest books when he was based on this side of the range so it is surprising to find no chapters, anywhere, on Lochnagar, though asides show he knew it as well as anywhere else. He left home to study at Oxford University, went on an expedition to Spitsbergen, visited Russia's forests but his heart was firmly set in the Cairngorms.

THE SNOWY CORRIE OF BEINN A' BHUIRD

High on Beinn a' Bhuird is a great snowfield, The Laird of Invercauld's Tablecloth, a prominent object from the main Deeside road as the traveller approaches Braemar. It sometimes remains unmelted throughout summer and autumn, as during the year in which I write (1970). This snow lies in the shelter of Coire an t-Sneachda, *the Snowy Corrie* which, in these changing times, has remained the undisturbed home of red deer and ptarmigan while bulldozed tracks scar some of its neighbours. Nearly 2,000 feet below the corrie the River Quoich flows through its glen towards the distant Atlantic before it joins the Dee, which flows in the opposite direction and enters the North Sea. [A major fault line, the upper Quoich flows south-west, a line that continues through the odd Clach Fhearnaig to pick up Glen Tilt.]

Glen Quoich is a splendid wood of natural Scots fir, some of the trees being several hundred years old. There are many open spaces between these trees and heather (ling) growing here is in distinguished bloom early in August.

On a mid-July day a friend and I climbed to the Snowy Corrie. We waded the ice-cold river and climbed near a clear burn that hurried in a series of small cascades from its birth-place in the snow above. We could see many red deer feeding in the corrie. As we watched them the sky darkened and clouds descended on Beinn a' Ghlo and the hills of Glen Shee. Rain began to fall and a peal of thunder came from the Dee Valley at Invercauld. In the rain and gloom we were cheered by the sudden sight of *Silene acaulis,* its small red flowers covering the whole of a large stone. The snow had earlier covered the plant and retarded its flowering by almost two months. At the edge of the snow the grass, although past mid-summer, was still brown and apparently lifeless but after a nine months' imprisonment beneath the snow the parsley fern (*Cryptogramma crispa*) was growing fresh green crinkled fronds. This rather uncommon mountain fern does have leaves with the appearance of parsley.

Violets are associated with spring or early summer, even on the hills, but in this high corrie the violets were only now flowering; small and pale blue, they hide themselves in the short, wiry grass. Near the roof of Scotland the curtain of rain now covered us, daylight faded and a thunder peal crashed overhead. The small burn, even at its source, was rising each minute and we thought of the river far below us and the effect of the thunderstorm on its water – it had to be forded on our return! The deer which had been feeding in the corrie earlier had moved as we approached but a half-grown calf had been left behind. It may have been asleep when the herd left and now, suddenly awakened and in a panic, passed at speed, covering the uneven ground downhill in a series of leaps and bounds. This deer calf was well able to look after itself but fawns when very young are sometimes abandoned by their parent.

In the Snow Corrie of Beinn a' Bhuird we later saw (still in torrential rain) a hen ptarmigan with her half-grown brood. The young birds had been sheltering under the boulders and accompanied by their mother, flew reluctantly only a short distance. Young ptarmigan have to be tough to survive on the high hills. One chick however had strayed so the mother, without slackening her speed, made a quick turn, flew back uphill, and called to the chick which rose at once and together they flew fast to join the rest of the family. Before we reached the glen 1,500 feet below we passed dwarf birch (*Betula nana*), growing in long heather and crowberry plants (*Empetrum*) with many black berries. The river was rising fast and looked formidable. My friend, springing like a chamois from rock to rock, crossed with the loss of his mackintosh. I took, as I thought, the safer way, wading where the river widened. The current was strong and the river bed uneven and without the steadying support of a strong stick I might have found myself following the mackintosh seaward. On the farther bank we rested and saw Cairntoul and Beinn Bhrotain free themselves from the clouds and watched the stony summit of Lochnagar light up as the sun reached them. High in the clear air a golden eagle was sailing, perhaps drying out his wings after the thunderstorm. As he rose still higher it was seen (through a telescope) that two small birds had risen to attack the giant. Time after time they attacked and the fact that they were house martins, far from their nesting eaves somewhere in the Dee valley, made the incident memorable.

Again the sky darkened to the north and heavy rain could be seen falling in the high corrie where the violets flowered. On the screes of Cairntoul cloud suddenly formed as the rainbearing north wind reached them. The golden eagle dislikes a wetting. He saw the approaching storm, half-closed his wings, and in a swift glide descended to the shelter of the old Scots firs.

HS-71

MORVEN IN SNOW

About six miles north-west of Dinnet, Morven, *the Great Hill* (2,863 feet) lies midway between the valleys of the Dee and Don, and from the summit cairn a view of surpassing beauty is obtained in every direction.

The new year is only a few days old but a succession of warm south-westerly winds has caused most of the traces of recent snow to disappear. Motoring from Aboyne, we have, at the old mill of Dinnet, to take the car through a field, as an immense drift, which a day or two ago was estimated at 20 feet in depth, lies across the road. The route is by Ordie and Loch Davan and two wreaths have to be cut through to reach Morven's base. The air is soft and mild and extraordinarily clear but a gale blows from the south-west and it is not easy to make progress against it.

One huge drift is noted in a low-lying corrie and the fence is completely hidden by the snow. The first white hare is seen just below the 2,000 feet level and he runs off looking for all the world like a small snow wreath as he is spotlessly white with the exception of his ears. Just before reaching the mossy plateau lying about the 2,000 feet line we put up several ptarmigan. These mountain dwellers are rarely met with below 2,500 feet but we have noticed them several times at this place, even during the nesting season, which is interesting seeing that on Lochnagar, Ben Muich Dhui, and their other strongholds they do not descend much below 3,000 feet. All round the plateau pack after pack of grouse get up and, rising against the wind, gradually swerve off and fly down-wind at express speed. The birds are exceptionally wild and take wing while we are several hundred yards from them.

Although it is only two o'clock the sky to the south-east, from Mount Keen to Kerloch, is lit up a beautiful pink, as though the sun has already set. Morven's southern slopes have many deep and soft wreaths on them but we strike off to the right and gain the summit plateau at the eastern cairn which is partly of natural formation. Before reaching the summit however we have some snow climbing as a drift some 200 yards along and exceedingly steep bars the way and at one point we are almost blown from our scanty footing by the force of the gale. On the distant wreaths coveys of grouse stand or run about, looking very comical on the snow, and a number of hares run quickly for safety. Several roosting hollows of grouse are discovered, some containing fresh droppings; a bed on the snow must prove rather chilly when there is so much bare ground.

As we emerge on the summit plateau the wind blows with hurricane force but after 400 yards we gain the shelter of the cairn and gaze our full at the view.

We have climbed Morven many a time but never has the view been such as to-day. Due south, Mount Keen (3,077 feet) and Braid Cairn, a few hundred feet lower, are comparatively free of snow. The summit of Clach-na-Ben is clearly seen, as are also Kerloch and Cairn Mon Earn. Evidently there is less wind further down the valley, for the smoke of Banchory is lying above the village and the North Sea is hidden by the smoke of Aberdeen. North and west supply the grandest view; due north, Ben Rinnes is bathed a glorious pink by the setting sun, north-west the blue is tinged with green which gradually merges into dark blue, and still further west the sky is tinged with pink. The Brown Cow (3,000 feet) between Gairn and Don, carries an immense drift on its south side, locally known as the Brown Cow's White Calf. To the north-west, about eleven miles distant, the road from Cock-bridge to Tomintoul is seen winding up the hill and filled with huge drifts. Ben Avon and Cairngorm are occasionally hidden by mist and at times the giant stones on the former's summit are the only part of the mountain left visible. Looking south-west, ice-bound Loch Muick is seen nestling amongst the mountains and Lochnagar and the Cuidhe Crom make a beautiful picture with the setting sun behind them.

Suddenly a mist envelops the cairn behind which we are sheltering and we see for the first time the shadow of Morven thrown on the clouds. All the time the mist rests on the summit a horse-shoe-shaped rainbow or 'glory' is outlined against the mist and for a few seconds a double mock rainbow appears. As the mist clears we notice the great distance to which the shadow of Morven extends. Even east of Towie many miles down the Don all is in shade and every moment as the sun sinks lower the shadow increases. About 3.30 the sun disappears beneath an Atlantic storm cloud on the horizon and the cloud's edges are for some minutes tinged with purest gold. Just as the sun is disappearing a covey of eight snow-white ptarmigan wheel across the hill from the Donside direction. As they reach the sunlight their snow-white plumage is suddenly lit up a rosy tinge.

A curious phenomenon is now visible, as from the eastern horizon three great rays gradually spread over the whole sky, one points south-east, another north, and the third north-west. The sunset has a marvellous effect in the valley of the Don, lighting up wood, field, and heather with a fiery tinge. The Bin Hill of Cullen, many miles to the north-east, has its full share, while Lochnagar against the sunset is a dark bluish-black. After lingering to look on this panorama we strike down the south side of the hill. We hoped to have been rewarded with some glissading but the snow is comparatively soft and after several unsuccessful attempts we have to give up. The grouse rise startled at our feet, calling loudly in alarm, and darkness rapidly descends on the mountain while the glow in the west becomes gradually fainter and fainter, until at last night reigns supreme.

BLM-07

THE COUNTRY OF BALMORAL

Balmoral, the Highland residence of the King [George VI] stands on the south bank of the River Dee eight miles east of Braemar. The lands of Balmoral extend southward to the dark massif of Lochnagar, a hill that was sung of by the poet Byron and is a landmark from near and far – from distant Aberdeen and from the low ground of Angus away to the south. The words written by Queen Victoria in her *Leaves from the Journal of our Life in the Highlands* when (in September 1848) she and Prince Albert looked for the first time on their future Highland home, were: 'All seemed to breathe freedom and peace, and to make one forget the world and its sad turmoils.'

In 1564 we find that Balmoral, in a charter of Queen Mary to the Earl of Moray, was part of the Earldom of Mar. In an old valuation dated 1635: 'Balmorall pertains to James Gordon of Balmorall'. Before the end of the seventeenth century Balmurell or Balmurrell came into the possession of Charles Farquharson of Inverey and half-brother of John, the Black Colonel – probably through an intermarriage with one of the Gordons of Abergeldie. Charles was succeeded by his nephew, James Farquharson of Balmurrell, who was 'out' in 1715 and 1745 and was severely wounded at the battle of Falkirk in 1746. The estates of Balmoral and Inverey then fell to the Farquharsons of Auchendryne. Towards the end of the eighteenth century a James Farquharson sold Inverey, Balmoral and Auchendryne to the Earl of Fife. Balmoral was later rented by Sir Robert Gordon, on whose death in 1847 the lease was acquired by the Prince Consort who bought the freehold five years later.

The magnificent old pine forest of Ballochbuie is part of the Balmoral estate. Here the trees have changed little since the days when wolves roamed the forest and kite and goshawk had their homes there. About the year 1907 I was shown by Charles Macintosh the nest of a kite in one of these old pines. The kite had then been extinct for upwards of forty years yet the nest, built in the fork of the tree, was still in a good state of repair.

The hill of Lochnagar, on 3,800 feet, is the highest ground of the Balmoral forest and takes its name from a small loch cradled deep in a corrie immediately beneath the summit. Professor Watson informs me the old Gaelic name is Loch na Gaire, *Loch of the Outcry*, with reference to violent wind.

Of Lochnagar Byron sang:

> *Years have rolled on, Lochnagar, since I left you,*
> *Years must elapse ere I tread you again;*
> *Nature of verdure and flowers has bereft you,*
> *Yet still are you dearer than Albion's plain.*
> *England! thy beauties are tame and domestic*
> *To one who has roved o'er the mountains afar:*
> *Oh for the crags that are wild and majestic!*
> *The steep frowning glories of dark Lochnagar!*

In summer a strange bird may sometimes be seen flying fast on scimitar-like wings backwards and forwards over the precipices of Lochnagar. Eagle and ptarmigan are at home here but to see the swift is unexpected yet swifts on still days of June and July often perform aerial evolutions on the hill. They are perhaps attracted from the glens by the insects which rise on the warm air currents but one observer has put it on record that he has seen a swift flying over the Lochnagar precipice with a straw in its bill and it is possible that the swift may at times forsake the steeples and castles and make its nest in some cranny of a precipice in the high hills.

Crathie church, where their Majesties worship when in residence at Balmoral, stands above the main road near the gates of Balmoral Castle but on the opposite side of the river. The foundation stone of the present building was laid by Queen Victoria in 1893; the earlier church is described in the *Old Statistical Account* as 'in very bad order and too small'. The pre-Reformation church was dedicated to St Manirus. The tradition of this saint is recorded in the Aberdeen Breviary, where we are told that in consequence of the difficulty caused by diversity of language (during the transition between Pictish and Gaelic), Manirus, being 'excellently skilled' in both languages, went to labour at Crathie in Braemar. Among the grave-stones in the churchyard of Crathie is one to John Brown, 'the devoted and faithful personal attendant and beloved friend of QUEEN VICTORIA in whose service he had been for 34 years.' [The stone has various quotations, typical of the period. When Queen Victoria was buried, a portrait of John Brown was placed in the coffin beside her.]

H&BC-48

ON THE DEE IN FEBRUARY

The frost of the past few days has 'louped' in the night, and the morning air is soft and mild. Along the valley of the Dee there is much activity for the river is opening its waters after the close season of winter. It is difficult to realize that winter has gone for there has been an almost entire absence of snow and little frost. Were it not for that unmistakable odour of spring given off by the humid earth it would be easy to imagine this a mild October day.

A narrow track, leading from the high road through a plantation of pines, brings us to the river bank. The water is too low for a successful opening this January. This season was dry and there is little or no snow on the hills to keep up the river. The line is wetted and, with that added interest of the unknown which must always mark the first day of each season, the first pool is fished carefully down, the fly a sober-coloured Glentana. At the head of the pool a couple of red-breasted mergansers are energetically fishing and three or four mallard rise from the water's edge, quacking huskily. No oystercatchers as yet people the long pebbly shingles (they arrive on the opening days of March) and no sandpiper flies twittering just above the river's surface. But water ouzels [dippers] fly and dive, and a sparrow hawk passes by at its hunting.

The first pool is fished down – not a fin showing – the second gives no better results and one's early enthusiasm begins to wane. But the best pool is close at hand and here at least, says the ghillie, there are fresh-run salmon in plenty and success is sure. A long deep pool this, spanned by a bridge near its middle, a strong current near the top of the pool, gradually slackening till, near the tail, in this low water, the river's motion is scarce perceptible. This pool is fished from a boat and on rowing up the head of the stream we pass, resting moribund near the water's edge, a diseased salmon with fungus growing thick on it. On the far side of the stream a fisherman on the opposite bank has landed a small silvery spring salmon, and up and down the pool fish break the surface of the water.

A few casts, then a tightening of the line – a false alarm, a small ice floe fouled the line in its passing. The temperature of the water this morning is only 33°F (one degree above freezing point!) and only a slight frost is needed to fill the river with floating ice or 'grue'. After a disheartening spell of unprofitable casting over waters apparently in perfect order a salmon at last rises to the fly (a white-winged Ackroyd) but he comes short and, in the slack water with a strong wind sagging the line, the hook is not driven home.

From this point onwards the pool seems full of fish. From the boat one can see them plainly in the clear depths, large 20-pounders and small spring fish of 6 to 8 pounds. But the water is too clear. Not a rise, save indeed where a fish, excited by the fly, leaps near it clear out of the water. The fly is changed no fewer than four times without result. The wind rapidly increases. In the pine wood above, the trees toss and sway, and the deep sighing of the wind is borne to us on the river. Casting becomes difficult for the wind blows now this way, now that, and the boat becomes hard to manage. To make matters worse the early afternoon sun breaks through the quickly moving clouds and shines brightly on the river.

This fine pool is given up for the day for its fish are obviously not on the take and a small pool just above is casted over. Almost at once a heavy fish takes the fly. Its appearance is doubtful but one hopes for the best and the fish, getting well away with the current, rushes clear out of the pool and down two hundred yards of heavy water before being brought to the shore. It is not until it has been tailed that the worst is confirmed – a heavy 20 lb kelt (spawned female) and so to be returned to its element; the angler by this time almost as exhausted as the fish itself.

The short February day is drawing to a close. The sinking sun is obscured by hurrying clouds, sweeping across from the north and gradually the hills are enveloped in mist.

About four o'clock the last pool, broad and placid, is reached. On it is swimming a tufted duck, not a common bird on the Dee – but not a sign of a fish. Half-way down the pool a faint touch – these early February salmon rarely rush at the fly like the late spring fish – and one is into a small and lively fish. Surely a clean salmon this time. Its strength is rapidly spent (a bad sign) and the fish turns out to be another kelt. This is the uncertainty of early fishing; one can never be sure whether the fish hooked is clean-run or not and, as a general rule, the kelts exceed the clean fish by three to one.

In the gathering dusk we prepare to leave the river bank. But with the last cast of the day a salmon, flashing across the pool, seizes the fly. They are both active and powerful, these small February fish, and it is not without a struggle that he is brought to the shore – a perfectly clean-run fish of 8 lbs.

WON-21

WINTER ON MOUNT KEEN

Few hills in Aberdeenshire stand out so prominently as Mount Keen (Monadh Caoin) *the beautiful hill*, 3,077 feet. Situated near the head of the Tanar, it forms the march between the forests of Glen Tanar and Glen Muick while its southern slopes lead down to the Esk. The morning chosen for the ascent dawns somewhat threateningly, with a very red sunrise, but when we leave Aboyne the frost is still hard and the day gives promise of turning out well. For the first few miles the motor makes good progress but in the upper reaches of the glen a good depth of snow covers the ground and the going is very stiff [for a 1912 model]. In the shelter of the wood there has been no drifting but on the open moorland the road for long stretches has been swept bare and big drifts piled across it in various parts. However, by dint of backing the car and rushing each wreath, we penetrate about a mile beyond the stalker's cottage at Etnach. Here the drifts become insurmountable so the car is left and we walk the remaining mile to where the path strikes up the hill.

The frost has evidently been exceptionally severe in these parts for we cross the Tanar on the ice (for quite long distances the burn is frost-bound) and strike up the hill. We flush numerous grouse and see rabbits in plenty, these latter being in a very weak state owing to the frost and snow. Soon we reach a point where the spindrift is being blown in clouds before the strong west wind. As we progress the drift becomes so blinding that it is difficult to see ahead and the small dog becomes very sorry for himself, having eventually to be carried by its owner. After reaching the 2,000 feet line the drift, strange to say, ceases, owing to the fact that nearly all the snow has already been blown away; but in one slight depression, just before the last steep climb the spindrift is blinding.

The north-east corries of the hill hold an immense quantity of snow and a well-defined cornice is visible. Where we are walking the snow has been blown into strange waves by the force of the gale and resembles nothing so much as the surface of a troubled sea. At this height animal life is practically non-existent but for a glimpse of a snow-white ptarmigan as the bird disappears over the corrie, flying with the gale. Apparently even at this height there has been a 'fresh' [thaw] recently for we note a good deal of clear black ice appearing beneath the snowdrifts. The snow, as a rule, is strong enough to bear us but occasionally one of the party falls through with unpleasant results.

The clouds have gradually been descending and now envelop the hill but we push on. The wind increases to a full gale and the frost is intense – one's moustache and hair frozen hard. We plod on eagerly on the lookout for that most welcome sight, the summit cairn. After several false alarms, lest we have gone off the line in the mist, the cairn looms through the cloud. Here the gale blows with such power that we are blown across to the leeward side and the small dog has a narrow escape from being hurled down the corrie. The stones of the cairn are heavily coated with ice and snow and we are glad to regain breath in their shelter. Fearing a snowstorm, we soon make a move for less exposed quarters and are urged forward by the wind down the hill. A few hundred feet below the cairn the mist suddenly opens and we see the Braid Cairn near us, to our east. A thick haze somewhat restricts the view but Morven's bulk can dimly be made out across the valley of the Dee. A good many white hares are put up and we see the tracks of a fox in the snow.

One of the party here has rather an unpleasant experience. Seeing a tempting wreath he glissades gaily down it but at its lower extremity the drift becomes as hard as iron and, losing control, he goes down at full speed, being brought up by the heather at the bottom. A number of stags are made out at the foot of a corrie and one poor animal runs off as best he can with a broken foreleg, but makes wonderful progress notwithstanding. On the steep hill-side over against us the peregrine has his summer home.

As we reach the lower ground the snow becomes quite soft and down in the valley a fresh has set in. Looking back, we see the cone of Mount Keen from time to time appearing from out of the clouds but soon a big heavy bank of mist rolls up from the west and shrouds the hill. On the return journey deer in great numbers are passed and a hind and her calf, unused to motors misjudge the speed of the car and have a narrow escape. Once past the stalker's house at Etnach, said to be a corruption for the Gaelic Aitionach, *abounding in juniper*, we soon leave the forest behind and reach our destination before darkness sets in.

COH-12

147

A GALE BY THE DEE

The westerly gale, grim and angry, rushed through the weeping birches on the Moor of Dinnet, scattering their bronze leaves like flakes of whirling snow. From the river Dee, leaping exultingly seaward with a deep roar, the gale caught the turgid waves and lifted them in spindrift, as an ocean gale might lift the manes of combers breaking on a lee shore. The Dee rose higher and higher. Beside Coilacreich the pine trees, shaken by the wind and undermined by the river waves, gradually lost their hold. They fell and were borne seaward in that irresistible flood, waving protesting branches as they were whirled from their home. Behind the hill described by the poet Byron as 'Moven of snow' a rainbow lighted as the sun broke through the storm wrack for a few minutes yet mist held the high slopes of 'dark Lochnagar' in the King's forest of Balmoral. At the Manse of Crathie, where white wagtails haunt the lawn during the season of migration, the Dee crept inch by inch over the lawn towards the house. When the moon rose and shone pale on this scene of storm the wind still roared through the Dee valley but next morning the scene had changed and the wind had gone to rest, clouds were dispersing and the Dee was falling back from flooded lands to its river bed.

ISNB-41

11

People of the Hills

Seton Gordon was lucky that when he headed into the hills he was taken under the wings of many great characters, the keepers and stalkers who knew the hill intimately at all seasons. They were Gaelic speakers and living in remote spots (Corrour bothy was even maintained in season), a world that would be changed utterly by successive World Wars. Thankfully he has immortalised this kindlier world and its tough but gracious people.

Living far removed from the great cities and often amongst all that is most admirable and grand in Nature the Highland stalker has a certain distinctive charm. He has lived out his quiet life in his glen with the big hills he knows so well sheltering his home from the fierce winter storms and his glen is his whole world. He is abroad in all weathers. In wild January blizzards he may be out on the high ground after hinds. When it is realized how rapidly a blizzard of dry, powdery snow from the north may descend on the uplying glens, obliterating every object more than a few yards distant, it is a matter of surprise how seldom the Highland stalker does go astray. I have never heard of a life being lost for a stalker has more intimate knowledge of the ground than any other man and, in summer, when the mist lies thick on the hill, he is able to guide the sportsman unerringly, not only to safety but also to that part of the ground where, with the particular wind which happens to be blowing, stags are likely to be found.

On the morning of December 26, 1906 the frost was intense and there was scarcely a cloud in the sky so that there seemed every prospect of a clear day to follow. Towards noon, however, a grey cloud appeared on the horizon, snow began to fall and continued without intermission for forty-eight hours, accompanied by a whole gale from the north. A number of stalkers went to the hill that morning but though many of them had to fight hard to regain their homes they all succeeded in reaching them safely before dark. All the same it was fortunate for them that the northerly wind had for some days previous to the advent of the great storm brought frost and snow squalls to the hill country so that the hinds had left the higher grounds for the shelter of the woods and were thus in more accessible quarters than usual.

In spring the stalker's work takes him rarely to the high ground except, maybe, to kindle a hillside where the heather, to his way of thinking, is too long to afford the best grazing for his deer, and it is not until the latter end of August that the heaviest work of the year begins.

Day by day before the 'gentlemen' are astir the stalker is closely scanning the corries through his glass and day after day, perhaps under a blazing sun, with no breath of air to cool the hillsides, perhaps in a heavy storm of rain and snow, he is abroad on the high grounds.

The Highland stalker sees many a fine sight: the battle between the sun and the mists, the coming of the cold north wind to the hills – the north wind which drives irresistibly the fine weather before it and which settles down on the hill-tops, carrying with it cloud and impenetrable gloom, he sees too the black eagle – the *Iolaire Dubh* of the hillman – and round the eagle he weaves many stories.

The hill stalker admires the eagle. A veteran hillman recently told me how he was taking notice of the nobility of the bird when mobbed by grey crows, the eagle continuing on its flight heedless of the repeated attacks of its small adversaries. A curious expression has been used in conversation with me on the soaring of the King of Birds, the stalker observing that he had seen the eagle "waving" in the sky.

I remember once when on the hill, a white-bearded stalker asking me whether I could name to him the 'Seven Sleepers of the Earth.' I learnt from him later that he considered the wheatear, (stonechacker he called it) was one of the seven and he treated my scepticism with something like pity. He described to me how he had discovered a hibernating wheatear at the end of a hole on an exposed moor. His story was evidently true but the weight of the assertion was lessened when he added that the bird was found in the month of March. It would thus appear that this wheatear was an early migrant which had sought refuge at the end of a burrow from the cold spell.

On one occasion he had followed a wounded stag to where it had fallen in a burn and as he was engaged in gralloching the beast he heard an object strike the water beside him with a splash. In surprise he raised himself quickly – to see a golden eagle check itself suddenly on its downward stoop and soar upwards, leaving a dead ptarmigan to float downstream.

Not so long ago I was lucky enough to come across a cairngorm stone of somewhat exceptional size while out on the high hills, and though the stalker rarely allowed his feelings to become evident, in this instance he was constrained to remark that I had indeed discovered "a brave stone". Another stalker, remarking on the weather experienced during that season, described how "at times the sun would gain the masterpiece, but then the wind would get up, and the mist would come down, and the atmosphere would become most ungenial." Talking of the expeditions of a certain ornithologist, he once remarked that "at times fine weather would accompany him" – an expression of charm when spoken by this old hillman in his characteristic way.

In a lonely bothy in the very heart of Scotland an old watcher took an interest in the birds near his solitary abode. On fine July days he would climb to the highest tops and would sit quietly watching the snow buntings entering and leaving their homes amongst the rough granite scree, "dancing on the hill in the sunlight." In the bothy field mice lived and my old friend used to spend the evenings in taming his small companions. After a time the mice even fed on crumbs which he placed on his boot, striking each other comically with their paws in their efforts to obtain as large a share as possible.

An experience which this old watcher had will bear setting down. On a July afternoon, after a day of sun and oppressive heat, a heavy thunder-cloud gathered above the hill north of the bothy. The air had the stillness which often precedes a storm and twilight descended on that part of the glen although the sun shone with curious red light at the head of the pass. Without warning, instantaneously, a solid mass of water struck the hilltop opposite the bothy with a deafening crash. A surging torrent immediately rushed tumultuously down the hill face, leaving a deep scar – visible at the present day – and bearing in its course rocks of such size as to be beyond the power of man to lift. A second wall of water descended on the hill above the bothy, the rush of water narrowly missing the small habitation and its solitary and shaken inmate. The storm soon passed, and the sun shone out but the debris washed down to the foot of the glen was so extensive that the river was held back and a lochan temporarily formed there.

During the spring meeting of a certain Alpine club on the Cairngorms, the ascent of Cairn Toul (4,241 feet) was attempted during a wild day, with a northerly gale and heavy snow squalls. The mountaineers encountered Arctic conditions on the hill and had to cut their way step by step up the precipitous face. Between the storms of snow they could be seen clinging like ants to the hill and finally reached the summit in a blizzard so terrific that they could scarcely draw breath. A stalker, after hearing full details of the climb, mildly stated "that he could well believe it was rather *airish* on the top."

At the fall of the year the hills surround themselves with the roaring of many stags. A fight in grim earnest between two stags is of rare occurrence but no stalker with whom I have spoken has ever witnessed a battle to the death. A veteran keeper had, indeed, on one occasion come across a stag still warm and bearing the marks of the antlers of his adversary where the fatal wound had been dealt.

When I first knew the Derry there were two fine old stalkers there. One of them Donald Fraser, lived in Derry Lodge, the other, John Macintosh, had his home in Luibeg Cottage. After John Macintosh came Sandy MacDonald, and after him Alick Grant, a piper and, in his younger days, a heavyweight athlete. Alick Grant's wife came of good Highland stock. Her father, John Stewart, a noted deerstalker of Atholl, accompanied Queen Victoria on her journey through Glen Tilt. Her eldest brother Peter was for many years head stalker to the late Duke of Atholl and the eldest sister was the wife of a well-known Highland deerstalker, Donald Crerar, Ardverikie.

The deerstalkers on the royal forest of Balmoral were all fine men. There was a rather curious custom that, when on the hill, the royal rank of the 'gentlemen' was temporarily forgotten, and they were addressed with a familiarity that would never have been thought of elsewhere. This familiarity was sometimes a shock to the ambassadors of foreign nations. I recall an ambassador of Spain hearing one of the stalkers say to the late King George V: "You will bide here (showing him a place of concealment) but there's the Laddie (the Prince of Wales); I dinna know what we will dae wi' HIM."

Charles Macintosh, second stalker on the Balmoral Forest, I knew well and often stayed with him. It was he who, by supporting my weight on a ladder which he raised and held against his chest, enabled me to take my first photograph of a golden eagle's eyrie when I was a boy. His wife, I remember, was the baker of some of the finest scones I have tasted. Charles was an expert salmon fisherman. When the Court was not in residence at Balmoral the salmon caught were sent by passenger train to London or Windsor. In May and June, when the weather was warm and clear and the river was low, Charles Macintosh did his fishing after sunset and before sunrise so that he had to be content with three or four hours' sleep, and sometimes less, of a night. Many a fine salmon have I seen him take from the river in the early hours of the morning when other folks were in bed and sound asleep. He was a great animal lover and in his time had some beautiful collies and deerhounds. I remember being on the hill with him and a particularly lovely collie bitch which he then had. We were sheltering behind a knoll – there was a strong wind blowing at the time – when we were surprised to see a dog fox coming towards us up-wind, sniffing the air and moving fast. The fox had almost reached us when he got our wind and reluctantly turned away. Charles said that he had known the same thing happen before, and had no doubt that the dog fox had got the bitch's scent and had been unable to distinguish it from the scent of a vixen in heat.

HY-44

In my own lifetime both bothies in Glen Eanaich have disappeared; the Corrour bothy, made more durable and strong, remains but has greatly deteriorated. It was used during the stalking season by a deer watcher who lived in it from Monday to Saturday. On Saturday he was accustomed to walk down to his home at Inverey, a walk of some eleven miles which included, at its beginning, the fording of the Dee, sometimes none too easy in times of rain. I often used to stay in the bothy while studying and photographing snow bunting and ptarmigan, and of the watchers I have special memories of two – Charles Robertson and John Macinstosh known as 'the Piper'. Charles Robertson was old when first I knew him but made light of the long walk each week-end. He had remarkable poise, and used to leap from one boulder to another when crossing the turbulent and flooded Dee, to the admiration of nervous spectators half his age.

Charles Robertson used to spend much of his spare time digging for crystals; he was also a keen fisherman. He was most hospitable and used to invite the traveller into the bothy for a cup of tea. In those days sweetened condensed milk was not a luxury neither was sugar rationed but everything had to be carried up on one's back from Braemar so his hospitality was admirable. He lived to be a very old man and was over ninety when he died. John Macintosh who succeeded him was a powerful man, slow and deliberate in thought and actions, a good naturalist and keen piper. He used to have his pipes with him at the bothy and sometimes on a dark night I was guided to his door by the strains of 'Donald Cameron', his favourite tune, which sounded loud and clear through the glen. I have pleasant memories of his piping as I sat beside a roaring fire of peat and bog fir, very grateful after a long walk on the hills. John Macintosh was an adept at kindling a fire swiftly. However early in the morning a start had to be made from the bothy he had the kettle boiling and a good breakfast ready. It was a cheery wee room with its old box bed.

Those were happy days. The Cairngorms have not changed, nor have even the old pines in Glen Luibeg during the last forty years (this seems to show that they are of a great age), yet the people of the glens, the old hillmen who knew by name each knoll, hollow and streamlet, have gone never to return. Houses are ruinous where courtly highlanders lived and those who remain are fast losing the old tradition. This is the tendency everywhere in the Highlands but it is specially marked in Mar. Think of old Charlie Robertson lighting his fire before dawn in the Corrour Bothy in order to walk through Lairig Ghru fifteen miles to Aviemore to catch the morning train to Inverness so that he might hear the leading pipers compete at the Northern Meeting. Think of the hill ponies, carrying the stags shot near the Wells of Dee, traversing the Lairig Ghru by the light of the moon or in inky darkness. The old stalkers have gone, and with them the Gaelic language which survived in Mar until after the close of the First World War and now only lives in the place-names of hill and corrie.

HOS-51

Alick Grant was deerstalker and piper in that great deer forest of Mar and his son Iain a keen naturalist. When Sandy MacDonald retired from the Derry, Sandy Grant took up his duties as stalker on that beat of the forest and he and his family moved to the stalker's cottage of Luibeg, just across the river from Derry Lodge. With them they took a pet crow, which had been reared by them as a fledgling a number of years before. The little party crossed the Derry river then, a few hundred yards farther on, crossed the Luibeg stream and the crow was given its liberty in its new surroundings. A day or two later the settlers crossed once more to the Derry (for the road up the glen does not go farther than that lodge) to bring over their belongings. The crow saw them leave and thinking that their stay in the new home might be only temporary flew with them across the two streams to the Derry. It returned when they returned, and from that day never crossed the streams. It met an untimely fate, being, as was supposed, killed by a weasel. The family mourned their pet which had been with them for twenty years.

HY-44

An old Highland stalker once gave me some of his experiences of the king of birds. Many years ago a pair of golden eagles had their eyrie on his beat and one season he was requested by the owner of the estate to capture the young eagles and bring them back as best he could. The eyrie was on a rocky hillside built on a ledge but after some difficulty it was reached and the eagles captured – by no means an easy undertaking – and placed in a large basket which the stalker had taken with him for that purpose. Just as he was preparing to leave, however, the parent bird appeared on the scene and proceeded to attack him in the most determined manner. Out of self-defence he or his companion fired at the infuriated eagle and after several shots she fell among the heather at the foot of the rock. The exact position was carefully marked and a detour having been made round the rock the bird was found lying to all appearance, lifeless on the ground. The stalker was preparing to lift her, with a view to placing her in his gamebag, when suddenly the bird came to life again and fixed her talons in the unfortunate keeper's arm, holding in an iron grip. It was some minutes before the bird could be persuaded to let go her hold. The talons had pierced right through to the bone, inflicting a severe wound. Although dressed with all possible skill the healing process was extremely slow and to this day the stalker bears the marks of the encounter with the eagle.

COH-12

A friend of mine, who owns a deer forest and protects his eagles, told me a tale about when he was travelling south from the Highlands. In the dining car that evening he sat opposite a stranger who in course of time entered into conversation with him and told him that he was pestered by – naming my friend's name – a certain gentle-man's golden eagles, which came over to his moors and alarmed his grouse. Then he confided to the stranger that he had got even with this man for he had pole traps set on his ground and had succeeded in capturing in them more that one golden eagle. Thus on his own showing he had twice broken the law of the land. Pole traps, because of the deadly pain they inflict upon the creatures they catch, are illegal and the golden eagle is also protected by law. My friend heard the unsavoury story out to the end but did not divulge his identity. He went to the chief constable of the county, and told him the story.

One saturday evening two old worthies boarded a local train and entered my compartment. They had both had a good dram. Before long a discussion started as to the wing-spread of the golden eagle. I ventured to agree with the opinion of one. He in the minority looked at me rather doubtfully and although he plainly thought I did not know what I was talking about he was too polite to say so. His friend, who I had seen eyeing the label on my luggage, said to him quietly, "Do ye know who yon is?" " No, indeed" came the answer. "Well," said the first in triumph, "yon is Setton Gordon!" This remark was rather a score for his convivial companion, remaking "A'm din" (I'm done), ceased to argue the subject. Sandy MacDonald was a grand old man, known as the Brogach, *the Lad*, who for many years was stalker on the Derry beat of

Mar Forest. When we lived at Aviemore Sandy walked through the Lairig Ghru to visit us. He had never seen the sea and took the train to Inverness to look at it but I remember that he was disappointed with his visit for the ocean as seen from Inverness is not inspiring. I recall crossing the Lairig one September day with my friend, Major L.F. Hay of the Forty-Second Highlanders. Major Hay was six feet eleven in height, the tallest man in the British Army. Sandy and the Prince of Wales (now Duke of Windsor) had been stalking and as we approached we saw them standing outside Sandy's cottage at Luibeg. The Prince came out to meet us (we both knew him well) and Sandy told me afterwards that they had been spying us through their stalking glasses when we were still a good distance away, and that the Prince had told him that Major Hay and he had been through the early part of the 1914–1918 war in France together, and that it was strange that Major Hay, the tallest man in the army should have been wounded in the foot. That day they had been stalking on the high ground of Ben MacDhui, and their stalk was spoiled by a tourist who gave the deer his wind. The Prince said to Sandy, "Shall I fire a shot a few hundred yards from him, Sandy, just to let him know there are stalkers on the hill?" "Na, na, Your Highness" relied Sandy "it would maybe get into the *Daily ——*," mentioning a newspaper of socialistic leanings. All the stalkers told me that the Prince was a first-rate shot with a rifle, better than his father King George V.

Shortly after the end of the 1914–1918 war, Sandy MacDonald found what he supposed to have been a bomb on the hillside behind his cottage. He took the object home and one day when the Prince of Wales was out stalking, he showed him the 'bomb'. The Prince sent it to the Air Ministry where it was recognised as a flare and was later found to have been dropped by Zeppelin L20 when over Mar Forest by night at the beginning of May, 1916.

HY-44

• • •

This had been reported on earlier.

On May 2nd, 1916 Zeppelin L20 left Germany under the command of Captain Lieutenant Stabert on a raiding voyage to Britain. The great aircraft crossed the coast at Lunan Bay, turned inland past Montrose then set her course for the Forest of Mar. From the little village of Inverey the menacing roar of its engines was heard by the stalking community. From the skylight window of one house a light showed that attracted the airship. She circled round in the darkness and, expecting momentarily a bomb to fall in their midst, the dwellers of that house were not long in darkening the tell-tale window.

But the Zeppelin passed on and sailed above Ben Mac Dhui to Spey, thence across the Monadh Liath range and the Caledonian Canal beyond. She crossed the North Sea and, driven against high land on the Norwegian coast on the morning of May 3, sank in the deep waters of a fjord.

[*The Scotsman 17.09.1924*]

• • •

The Cairngorms saw strange sights during the Second World War. They saw bearded Indians riding across their foothills and up to their high tops [see also page 7]; they saw Norwegian ski-troops, hardy and bronzed, on the their high plateaus at midwinter; they saw British climbers of the Mount Everest expedition camping in blizzards which, they said, exceeded in fury anything they had experienced on Everest; they saw mock battles with live ammunition fought on high ground with the eagle and the ptarmigan as the only spectators; they even, perchance, heard the famous order given that tanks should traverse the Lairig Ghru from Aviemore to Braemar. It is said that the tanks did indeed set out and their track through Rothiemurchus was visible for many a day but they had to confess themselves beaten on the higher rock-strewn slopes of the pass.

One of our own planes met disaster on Ben MacDhui and its crew were killed. The *Oxford* was ill-fated, for twenty feet more of altitude would have seen it safely over the hill. It crashed so close to the summit that it actually slipped across the watershed. There was close mist at the time; indeed the accident was not discovered until the cloud lifted and a climber saw a small column of smoke ascending into the sky near the hilltop. Another air disaster was not discovered until months later. An aircraft manned by a Czech crew crashed near the summit of Ben A'an in very lonely country during a winter blizzard. It was only late in the following summer when the victims were found and were buried at the head of a wild corrie – a fitting resting-place for airmen. The bodies were later exhumed, a difficult task, and taken away.

I met a Norwegian at the Juvasshytte, beside Norway's highest hill, Galdhöppigen (8,200 feet), in the summer of 1947, and he told me that he did much of his army training on the Cairngorms during the war and looked back with great pleasure to his days on skis on the high plateau 4,000 feet above the sea where the snow lay yards deep, the lochs were invisible beneath ice and snow and the conditions were truly Arctic. Many of our allies have pleasant recollections of the Highlands of Scotland and of the friendliness and hospitality of their people. Our own wartime soldiers, many of them city dwellers, also have these good memories. Some of them will remember with pride how they trained under Lord Rowallan, now the Chief Scout, in one of the Cairngorm glens on the intensive courses for potential officers. Lord Rowallan asked me if I would take some of these young soldiers up to the high Cairngorms to tell them of the plants, flowers and birds to be found there and we did a number of climbs in magnificent weather. We nearly caused strained relations with our Norwegian allies on one occasion by driving up to their headquarters where, we were told by an irate officer, we had no business to be. The Norwegians shared a shooting lodge with a deerstalker who on several occasions was held up because he could not give the password but, with true Highland independence, he refused to submit to these infringements on his liberty – and he had his way.

This reminds me of the predicament of two officers who were walking to dine with the King and Queen at Balmoral Castle. The Lovat Scouts were at the time guarding the castle and the two officers (not Lovat Scouts) had been given the password which they had forgotten. They were challenged by the sentry and, since they could not give the password, he insisted on their being brought before the officer of the guard – to the detriment of their smart uniform and burnished shoes, as they had to walk through long wet grass. When they arrived at Balmoral, late for dinner, it was necessary, in order to explain matters, to give an account of the incident which, rumour had it, greatly amused their host and hostess.

During those war years something like a spy mania swept over certain districts of the Highlands. One day the Registrar-General for Scotland [James Gray Kyd], a keen mountaineer, alighted at Aviemore platform during the change of engines at that junction and was enjoying the view of the Cairngorm hills when the stationmaster, seeing him studying a map, politely but firmly escorted him to his office and it was not until he had been shown the suspect's identity book and visiting card that he consented to release him.

HOS-51

12

A Varied Wildlife

In the world Seton Gordon knew so well deer – and stalking – dominated in the forests of the Cairngorms so he, perforce, wrote much about red deer. He also wrote about roe deer, wildcats, hares, otters and much else but his notes on the last wolf in Scotland had to be included and, last, though not about animated life, is a piece on Cairngorm Stones.

THE RED DEER OF OUR HILLS

Stalkers out after a hind in January find the crested tit a cheery companion. The size of a blue tit, he is a hardy little fellow and remains winter and summer in the Old Caledonian Forest. When a hind has been shot crested tits quickly appear. They love fat and when the hind is gralloched they fly down and fearlessly feed upon any suet or fat which lies on the ground.

ITH-31

The biting deer fly or cleg, one of the family of *Tabanidae*, was found high that day and I was bitten while on the shoulder of Cairntoul at 3,750 feet, a greater elevation than I have ever seen these pests. No doubt they followed up the stags which, later, I watched at the edge of a peat hag. The flies were causing the deer considerable discomfort and their long, flexible ears were continually being moved, so that for a time they hung for a brief second pendulous. They rolled in the wet peat, they shook themselves like dogs and when at last I had, perforce, to show myself to continue my journey, the startled herd gathered together and made off at their best speed.

How high do red deer live in summer in Scotland? They rarely climb to the highest hilltops. I doubt if a stag has ever been seen on the top of Ben Nevis nor do I ever remember seeing red deer on the summit of Ben MacDhui. In the finest summer weather deer are seen feeding on the green grass of Braeriach beside the Wells of Dee, 4,000 feet above sea level, but they are almost always hinds. Hinds feed higher than stags in summer. I have known one drop her calf on Braeriach 3,600 feet above the sea. Deer sometimes climb high in summer in order that they may lie or play on the cool surface of some snowfield.

HY-44

October is the mating season of the deer. At dusk I have heard the crack of antler against antler as two stags rush on one another. The fight is usually broken off before much damage has been done but I have heard of instances when the vanquished beast has been found dead or dying. Scrope mentions a particularly savage conflict that was fatal to both stags: 'Two large harts … after a furious and deadly thrust, had entangled their horns so firmly together that they were inextricable, and the victor remained with the vanquished. In this situation they were discovered by the forester, who killed the survivor whilst he was yet struggling to release himself from his dead antagonist. The horns remain at Gordon Castle, still locked together as they were found.'

Through October days and nights the hoarse challenge of stag to stag echoes through Highland glens, voices sometimes deep, sometimes cracked and hoarse. The unseen rivals listen for the reply to a challenge and, after roaring, run a little way in the direction of the answering cry. When they come in sight of one another the speed of the advance is accelerated, or one of the animals, not liking the looks of his opponent, gives ground slowly and with what dignity he can muster.

It is not difficult to mimic a stag's roar or draw an answering roar. I have often brought a beast near but usually the stag becomes suspicious and sheers off or else circles round to get wind of the object of his suspicions. When he has got one's wind that is the end of the whole business for when he scents man this spells danger to him with a big D and he takes precipitate flight. The roar of a hill stag brings back to my mind autumn days of long ago on the hill – days when the mist swept low across Carn a' Mhaim, and spread an impenetrable curtain over Ben MacDhui and Braeriach, when the moon, breaking through the cloud and shining on Glen Lui, bathed the old pines which seem everlasting as the hills themselves. For a time there would be silence and then, out of the mist would come the hoarse challenge from an invisible stag and perhaps the dark antlered form of his rival would be seen as he crossed the path ahead, his hinds respectfully following him.

Stags rarely have to use their gift of swimming yet they can if necessary swim far and well. They have been seen more that once swimming the tide-swept strait which separates the Isle of Mull from the mainland of Morvern. That icy strait is a couple of miles wide so they should find no difficultly crossing the sea from Skye to the mainland where the passage is less than a mile.

HY-44

In a well-known grassy glen where hinds are found throughout the year the big stags assemble to fight out their battles in early October. On one such night I happened to traverse the glen. In the darkness two voices especially could be distinguished. One stag I knew from his hoarse cries, a fine beast whom I had watched on previous occasions and when I last saw him was master over forty hinds. Across the glen from him a second stag was roaring with fine musical voice and as I moved forward, this stag, with his attendant hinds, stampeded across in the darkness right in front of me, making straight for that part of the hillside whence came the hoarse roarings of the big stag. From what I had seen I imagined he would drive off this trespasser on his ground with no difficulty. In the darkness nothing could be seen of the fight that followed but I could hear the striking of horn against horn. After a short time the fighting ceased; but the hoarse roaring of the big stag was silent and the deep calls of his rival coming from the spot where he was formerly heard seemed to point to the fact that the master had met his match.

On another occasion, a little earlier in the year the big stag had rounded up his hinds on a grassy hill face, while he himself was feeding quietly a considerable distance above them. As I watched, a smaller stag, who had been loitering near, approached the hinds but was immediately perceived by the lord of the herd. I do not think I have ever seen a stag cover the ground so rapidly as did this big beast as he charged down the hillside. The young stag cleared off immediately but although he had a good start the old warrior was not content until he had caught up and prodded him vigorously in the rear with his antlers.

One day in this forest I was witness of an extremely interesting occurrence. Near each other were two stags, both heavy beasts with fine heads, but one animal slightly superior in weight to the other. The heavier stag had the larger following of hinds and it was evidently his intention to round the hinds of his rival into his own herd. Though he had a slight advantage in weight he hesitated to force a fight and so time and again the two stags paced slowly across the hillside, often only a few feet distant from each other. The heavier beast roared repeatedly in the endeavour to intimidate his rival, sometimes walking close behind him, as though debating the advantages of a bold charge but on each occasion coming apparently to the conclusion that the results might be somewhat unpleasant for himself. By a certain amount of manoeuvring, however, he succeeded in rounding in his rival's hinds, one by one, until at length only a single hind remained to the stag who had thus been morally defeated. For a time he succeeded in keeping his last remaining wife with him but she too went across to the others in the end. When I last saw the unfortunate stag he was moving slowly and alone over the ridge to the hills beyond.

WON-21

SCOTTISH WILDCAT

Had it not been for the Great War of 1914–1918, it is probable our wild cat would be extinct. In the summer of 1914 it was on the verge of extinction, for by then it had been banished from Scotland except from a very few glens in the Central Highlands. During that war stalkers and gamekeepers left their homes and their vocations in order to serve in the Lovat Scouts, Cameron Highlanders, Black Watch, Scottish Horse and other Highland regiments, and when those who escaped death returned after the war they found that wild cats had greatly increased during their absence. And now the conditions of the war are again being experienced; the wild cat, which during the intervening peace years had held its own and even extended its range, must now increase still further.

Since the wild tom mates on occasion with the domestic cat there are many crosses in the Highlands and reports on the taming of so-called wild cats refer often to these crosses or even to domestic cats gone wild. (The tail of the true wild cat is thick to the tip, the tail of the cross tapers). A man with great experience of wild cats tells me that there is one infallible guide – the intestines of the wild cat are twice as long as those of the tame cat. The wild cat is the only British animal which no man has succeeded in taming. People who have kept them in captivity tell me that they are quite untameable.

One day a friend placed a mouse in his wild cat's cage, thinking that it would be appreciated but to his astonishment the cat uttered a shriek of terror and fled around and round the cage away from the mouse. When he placed a small bird in the cage it was seized and eaten at once.

A friend of mine came upon a family of wild cats in a grassy hollow through which a hill burn flowed. A rowan tree grew in the hollow and approaching the place quietly he saw that a family of wild kittens were amusing themselves by climbing the tree. One kitten would playfully cuff a companion off the tree then the two, falling to the ground, would roll over and over, biting and clawing one another in play. After watching the kittens for a time my friend threw a small stone into the tree. The kittens immediately ceased playing and looked intently all round them yet never thought of looking up. Very soon they forgot their alarm and played as energetically as ever. My friend then dropped a larger stone on to the tree. The kittens, more alarmed, froze, running down the tree and concealing themselves in the grass and heather. One by one they rose to their feet, climbed the tree again and the fun was renewed. Perhaps half an hour later my friend saw the mother of the family approaching. In her mouth she carried a rabbit and, although the human observer remained motionless, she either smelt him or in some other way sensed his presence for she dropped the rabbit and ran.

On another occasion, in the same glen, a motor car was passing along the narrow road after dark. Its headlamps showed a large wild cat on the road. The animal, apparently bewildered by the brilliance of the lights, actually sprang on to the roof of the car, from which, with a second leap, it disappeared into the darkness.

Audrey and I had a hiding-place of heather in position near an eagles' eyrie. One winter's day when the ground was snow-covered the stalker happened to pass near and, anxious to see how it was standing the winter storms, was about to lift the wire 'door' at the back when he heard a scraping noise within and saw a wild cat spring through the hole left for the camera in the front of the hide!

I once asked another Highland stalker whether he agreed that the wild cat was untameable. He said that an adult cat certainly was yet he believed that if a newborn wild kitten were handled by human hands *before* its eyes were open it might be tamed. So far as he knew, that experiment had never been made because of the difficulty of finding a wild cat's family at that very early stage. He had had a good deal of experience of crosses in his own glen as house cats frequently had families by wild toms. These kittens became excellent mousers and ratters and could be domesticated provided they were handled *before their eyes were open*: otherwise they grew as wild almost as the true wild cat.

One day as I approached an old pine stump, almost white from much bleaching by wind and sun, I metaphorically rubbed my eyes for I saw a light grey object moving on the top of that stump – the bushy tail of a wild cat. The tail quickly disappeared and on walking to the stump and striking it I found that it was hollow throughout its length. I believe the wild cat who had her home in the stump was about to set out on her night's hunting when she heard my footsteps approach and remained poised in the act of leaving the tree. When she saw me coming too close for her peace of mind she decided to re-enter her sanctuary and her tail, held stiff and erect, betrayed her alertness before she finally disappeared.

A Highland keeper had an even stranger experience. He was trying to climb to a peregrine's eyrie and had reached a grassy ledge a few feet below the eyrie when, to his amazement, a wild cat sprang from the ledge, missed its footing, and fell to the ground 70 to 80 feet below. It fell curved like a hedgehog half rolled up and he thought that this attitude was assumed deliberately for, when it reached the ground, the cat was on its feet at once and ran off. A fall of that height would have been fatal to a dog. He thought the wild cat had climbed to the ledge in order to carry off or feed on prey dropped from the peregrine's eyrie; the eyrie itself was inaccessible.

Wild cats are more destructive to game than foxes, for they kill for the mere lust of killing. A keeper on Braemore in 1939 tracked a wild cat in snow for a distance of about three miles and in that distance the cat had killed two rabbits, one hare and one grouse, without eating any of them.

ISNB-41

THE LAST WOLF IN SCOTLAND

Where was the last wolf slain in Scotland? More than one Highland district claims that honour and it is difficult for us to realize the horror the Highlander had of the wolf. Great areas of natural pine were burned for the sole reason that wolves had their home in the forest and made raids from its shelter. Many place names throughout the Highlands commemorate the wolf. By the sixteenth century the determined warfare waged against this animal was having its effect and the wolf had already been wiped out in certain districts.

In the *Wardlaw Manuscript*, written by Master James Fraser, Minister of the Parish of Wardlaw (now called Kirkhill) near Inverness, in the year 1666, we learn a little of this campaign. In the middle of the fifteenth century, Lord Hugh Lovat married Margaret, daughter of Lord Glamis, a lady 'singular for courage and magnanimity ... This Lord Hugh's lady was a stout, bold woman. A great hunter, she would have travelled in our hills afoot, and perhaps outwearyed good footmen. She purged Mount Capplach of the wolves: there is a seat there called Ellig ni Baintearn, (*the wolf trap of the lady*).

The present Lord Lovat tells me that when he was a small boy his father used to point out to him a spot in Glen Convinth (in the district mentioned in the *Wardlaw Manuscript*) where the last wolf was killed and a stone on the roadside commemorated that event. He estimates that the wolf was slain about the year 1700. In *Lays of the Deer Forests (Vol. II)*, written by the Sobieski Stuart brothers, it is narrated that a scar on this stone is the result of a stroke of the spear with which Chisholm of Chisholm slew the wolf.

William Mackay of Inverness, who has much knowledge of Highland lore, informs me that about this time a wolf was killed on the south shore of Loch

Duntelchaig, on the high ground about ten miles south of Inverness. It appears that the good-wife of MacGillivray of Dalchrombie one winter day was on her way to a neighbour's house to borrow a girdle to bake scones. The ground was snow-covered. As she was returning with the girdle she saw in the snow the tracks of a wolf which must have followed her on her outward journey. The wolf suddenly appeared and sprang at her. She swung her girdle, and cracked the animal's jaw, killing it instantly. This event, Mackay thinks, took place early in the eighteenth century. Ian Fraser of Reelig tells me that in the *Records of Inverness* there are one or two mentions of domestic animals being killed by wolves in the fifteenth century and that, as late as 1579, a legal reprimand was given to an Inverness burgh cottar for failing to keep his bestial 'fra thieff, wolf, pot and myre'.

It has been claimed that the honour of slaying the last wolf in Scotland should be given to MacQueen of Polochaig, 'a man nearer seven than six feet'. The wolf was killed beside the River Findhorn not far from Moyhall, the seat of Mackintosh of Mackintosh. A woman, crossing from the Findhorn valley with her two children to Moy, had been attacked and her children killed. Mackintosh, on hearing of this, instantly sent word to all his tenants in the district that they were to meet him the next morning in order to take part in a great wolf hunt. By the appointed hour they had all arrived, except MacQueen. The chief awaited him with growing impatience. When, an hour late, he appeared with his deer hound, Mackintosh unbraided him before the gathering. MacQueen stood in silence until his chief had finished speaking then slowly unwrapped his plaid, revealing to the gaze of all present the gory head of a huge wolf. He said that on his journey across the hills to Moy he had met the wolf on steep, rocky ground above the River Findhorn. He paused in his narrative, 'It was either him, or me,' he said. Again he paused. 'It was him,' he said firmly and solemnly. The slaying of that wolf, it is said, was in the year 1743.

On an autumn day of rain and wind, the River Findhorn rising fast and already in spate, I visited the lonely glen where that wolf had its home. The scene in the gathering dusk is impressed on my mind because my guide was Mackintosh of Mackintosh, direct descendant of the chief who figures in the story and on our way we met and conversed with the direct descendant of MacQueen who killed the wolf.

Lochaber in the West Highlands also claims the honour of the destruction of the last wolf. Sir Ewen Cameron of Lochiel, who was born in 1629 and died in 1719, was a great hunter as well as being a distinguished soldier. The *Memoirs of Lochiel*, 1842, state that Sir Ewen 'killed with his own hand the last wolf that was seen in the Highlands'. In Lochiel's castle at Achnacarry I have seen the flintlock with which Sir Ewen is said to have shot the wolf.

About the year 1880 the Gaelic poetess, Mrs. Mary Mackellar, helped in the writing of a volume entitled *MacDougall's Guide to Fort William, Glencoe and Lochaber*. In it she describes the killing of the last wolf Loch Eil-side in the sixteenth century on the hill above Corriebeg. It seems that a woman had gone to this hill for firewood and had there met the wolf: 'With great presence of mind she wrapped her tartan screen around her hand, leaving the fingers free, and held out her arm towards him. He grasped it eagerly, fixing his teeth in the part which was protected. Having her fingers free, she laid hold of his tongue, which she did not let go until she tore it out, and the wolf fell dead at her feet.'

It is noteworthy that Sir Ewen Cameron of Lochiel, the conqueror of the last Lochaber wolf, is said to have killed the last wolf in Perthshire also. In the Perthshire traditions that event took place in 1680 in the Pass of Killiecrankie. It is on record that no fewer than five wolves were slain in the Forest of Atholl in 1564 during a great deer hunt in honour of Mary Queen of Scots.

In Sutherland, which has always been a wild and sparsely-inhabited county it is likely that the wolf lingered long. John George Mackay who has his home at Achriesgill near Kinloch Bervie told me the tradition of the last wolf hunt in the north-west of Sutherland. That wolf was slain in a cave in Strath Dionard. The cave is known to this day as Uaimh Mhadaidh-alluidh, *Cave of the Wolf.* Near it rises Cnoc Mhadaidh-alluidh, *Knoll of the Wolf.* The story is that this wolf had killed a choice bull calf near Durness from the herd of Iain Mor, *Big John.* The tracks were followed in deep snow from the coast through Strath Dionard to the cave where the wolf was found. In the same district the place-name Fasach nam Faoil, *Wilderness of the Wolves*, must commemorate a special haunt: a district of boulders, deep ravines, and jagged rocks near the cliffs of Loch Dionard.

The story of the Strath Dionard wolf is not known widely and on that account is the more interesting. Indeed it is generally supposed that the last wolf in Sutherland, or indeed in all Scotland, was killed on the east coast, beside the road from Brora to Helmsdale. The event is commemorated by a cairn near the road at Loth. It is said that a hunter named Polson came upon a family of young wolf cubs in a cave. The hunter entered the cave and set about killing the young wolves with his dirk, while his son kept watch at the mouth of the cave. The agonized howls of the wolf cubs brought the mother wolf and as she was on the point of entering, young Polson seized her by the tail. From within his father called out in Gaelic, 'Co dhorchaich an toll?'; in English, 'Who darkens the hole?' His son replied in rhyme, translating,

'If the tail breaks/Your head will know/Who darkens the hole.'

The lad held on bravely and his father was able to slay the mother wolf, the last of her race, we may infer, in the British Isles.

HD-63

CAIRNGORM STONES

A Cairngorm crystal, or stone, is a hexagonal quartz crystal, coloured with oxide of iron but allowing the light to pass through when polished. In almost every jeweller's shop one can buy Cairngorm stones, quarried, perhaps, in some mountain range of Germany or Austria or even farther afield yet bearing the local name and difficult to distinguish from the crystals of the Cairngorms. There are doubtless many fine stones still in the corries and on the plateaus of the Monadh Ruadh but they are much scarcer than a century ago for shepherds and stalkers have searched diligently for them and the rarer precious stones beryl or aquamarine, a beautiful crystal of a deep blue colour that is very seldom found on the Cairngorms.

In the *Old Statistical Account* of Scotland, published in 1795, one reads the following:

> Some of the mountains (in the united parishes of Crathy and Braemar) are probably the highest in Scotland. Upon these mountains there is snow to be found all the year round and their appearance is extremely romantic and truly alpine. On them are found pellucid stones, of the nature of precious stones, equally transparent, beautiful in their colour: and some of them, particularly the emerald, as hard as any oriental gem of the same kind. The most common are, the brown, of different shades, and next the topaz. There are also beautiful amethysts and emeralds, though these are rare to be met with, particularly the latter; and what is remarkable, amethysts are only to be found in Loch-na-Garaidh; emeralds, topazes, and the brown on Binn-na-baird; topazes, and the brown, kinds

only on Binn-na muick-duidh and the other mountains
in these parishes. The first of these stones that attracted
notice, and were cut by lapidary, were found on Cairngorm, in Strathspey, but connected with the above ridge
of mountains, which gave rise, though very improperly,
to the general name of Cairn-gorm stones.

When crossing the plateau of Brae Riach or walking on the windy slopes of Ben
MacDhui or Cairn Toul I have frequently come upon circular holes of various sizes
and scattered around them lie blocks of quartz, broken with hammer or pickaxe
when, at different times, stalkers and shepherds have dug for the elusive Cairngorm.

Old Charles Robertson, for many years watcher at the Corrour bothy, searched
assiduously for Cairngorm stones in his spare hours. On one occasion he and
another stalker were crossing the face of Monadh Mor. There was a deer drive in
Glen Giusachan that day, at which the late King Edward [VII] was present, and the
two stalkers were hurrying, when suddenly they saw some fine Cairngorm crystals
peeping above the ground in the sand beside a small burn. There was no time to
dig out the crystals but the spot was hastily marked and a few days later Robertson returned thinking to find the stones. No trace of them could be seen, nor were
subsequent searches more profitable. Thus the Cairngorm crystals of Monadh Mor
lie undisturbed to this day.

I remember finding, near the top of Ben MacDhui, a fine crystal with its hexagonal point showing above the surrounding gravel. Hundreds of climbers – for Ben
MacDhui is a popular hill – must have passed close to or even over the stone without
seeing it. This was a lucky find for the best crystals now are discovered by digging.

It is said by those skilled in the art that when searching for the crystals it is
necessary to follow a quartz vein to where it disappears beneath the surface of the
hill and there to commence digging operations. Quartz veins are not uncommon
on the Cairngorm Hills but most of the likely spots have already been examined
and some magnificent crystals discovered. One such so heavy that it can be lifted
with difficulty, is at Invercauld House, another upwards of fifty pounds in weight,
was bought by Queen Victoria for £50. This crystal was found by one James Grant,
from Rebhoan in Glen More. He came upon it in a hollow among the rocks in an
east-facing corrie of Cairngorm. On cleaning out the hollow, which was filled with
sand, Grant discovered a number of splendid crystals. That was many years ago, but
the pot from which the crystals were taken is still clearly visible. During ten months
of the year that part of the hill is under snow.

Cairngorm stones are sometimes found in the bed of a burn and I remember one
being taken from the waters of Alltan na Beinne of Beinn a' Bhuird. I was told that
on one occasion some searchers for Cairngorm stones were defeated by water rising

in the hollow they had dug. This was beside one of the high streams of Ben Mac Dhui where much digging had revealed crystals firmly embedded in the rock but the water rose over them and the most strenuous bailing made no impression on it. And so the crystals await some future searcher.

But Cairngorm crystals do not always grow upon solid rock. The finest nest I ever discovered was in reddish clay, very soft and sticky. In this clay the crystals were lying free and resembled at first glance stunted and long-discarded lead pencils. Sometimes on the hills one finds crystals unstained by oxide of iron; these are not Cairngorms stones and of little value.

Nearly a hundred years ago an old woman might have been seen day after day on the High Cairngorms. Each burn, watercourse and corrie of Cairngorm and Ben MacDhui she searched for, at her home in the lowlands of Banff, she had dreamed of finding a precious stone on the hill.

At this time there was a legend that a wonderful crystal grew on some niche of the precipice that rises from Loch A'an. Shepherds and stalkers had seen it sparkle when the full moon threw her cold beams upon the cliff but it could not be found, possibly because the rock here was too steep for the most skilled climber. The tales of this precious stone had perhaps reached the woman in her distant home and had caused her to dream the dream that impelled her to travel westward and spend many days of the summer months sleeping out on the hills or beneath the Shelter Stone. She searched persistently and at last discovered a splendid beryl. Since in the Cairngorm Hills the beryl is a much rarer stone than the Cairngorm, the old lady's perseverance was well rewarded. The discovery so delighted her that for years after A' Chailleach nan Clach, *the Old Woman of the Stones*, continued to search the hills she by this time knew so well, and found many other crystals, of which the great stone at Invercauld House is, I believe, the largest.

CHS-25

Precious stones are much more difficult to find than when that was written for many people since then have searched carefully for them and remains of primitive, shallow quarries are often observed by the climber.

H&BC-48

13

Folklore of Spey and Dee

From his earliest days Seton Gordon was interested in people and obviously socialised easily, gathering stories of the ancient families, historical interlopers (armies, caterans, refugees) and a time when history is lost in folklore. For better or for worse we are the dominant species, the only one with this indulgence, this equivocal blessing. We are fortunate that Seton Gordon was as curious about the past as he was in observing the present.

NORTHERN ASPECTS

Most of the old Highland families had a being of some kind closely attached to them. The Shaws of Rothiemurchus sheltered a sprite named Bodach an Duin – the *Old Man of the Doune*. When the Grants took possession of the property Bodach an Duin left the house and from that time onwards guarded the tomb of the Shaws in Rothiemurchus burial ground. The Grants of Tullochgorm had also their tutelary being, in the form of a small boy, Mag Molach, *Hairy*, because his left hand 'was all over hairy.' On a dark night Mag Molach (or Meg Mulloch) would hold a candle before the Goodman and show him the way home. He was an autocratic being for if the Goodwife was dilatory in going to bed he 'would cast her in beyond him.'

Fifteen miles down the Spey from Aviemore is Grantown-on-Spey. The town is on the north bank of the river; above stands Castle Grant, once named Freuchie, for at least six centuries the home of the chiefs of Clan Grant – ever since Sir John Grant in the thirteenth century received as a gift from the King of Scotland part of the lands of Strathspey formerly held by the Cummings. It was first named the Castle of Grant in the year 1694. One of the towers, Lady Barbie's Tower, is said to be haunted by the ghost of Lady Barbara or Barbie, who was walled in alive there. In the castle is a striking portrait of the family piper, dated 1714. The story goes that this piper marched, playing all the way, from Inverness to Castle Grant, a distance of more than thirty miles, perhaps for a wager. He was approaching Castle Grant and was already being acclaimed by those who had gathered to see his arrival, when he staggered, his pipes wailed their last, and he fell dead.

HOS-51

Rothiemurchus and Glen More were renowned for the size and quality of the Scot firs that grew here. The trees when felled were floated down the Spey to the distant North Sea.

It is said that two families of the Grants had the honour of guiding the first trees from Glen More to the sea. This historic cargo consisted of eight logs fastened together by a rope made of horsehair. Ahead of the logs one or two men paddled a rudely built canoe or curach to steer the cargo, while other men, on either bank of the river, controlled the movement of the trees by means of ropes attached to the hinder part of the mass. Once in the Spey the logs floated quickly so the floaters were not long in reaching the sea. The return journey was more arduous, for each canoe was always carried on the back of its owner from the sea to Glen More, a distance of over 60 miles. One celebrated floater went by the name of Alasdair Mor a' Churaich, *Big Alastair of the Canoe*. The curach is now unknown in Scotland but in the west of Ireland the Aran Islanders are still skilled in its use.

There is a tradition that a curach from the Spey once performed nobly on the Thames. The Laird of Grant, on a visit to London, happened to speak admiringly to an English friend of the River Thames with its endless variety of sailing craft. The Englishman in a disparaging manner remarked, "You have, I suppose, nothing like that on your puny Spey." Instantly the proud highlander made answer, "I have on the Spey a subject who, in a boat of bullock's hide, would outstrip in speed the fastest of these craft." A wager was thereupon taken and the laird called upon a lad of eighteen from the Grant of Tulchen. This lad walked the 600 miles from Spey to London, carrying with him his favourite curach. Oars and sailing craft were pitted against him, but he easily outstripped them all and won the wager for his delighted chief.

CHS-25

In bygone days Glen More was the home of a fairy of immense stature, Domhnall Mor Bad an t-Sithein and *Big Donald* played many pranks so was not always popular. Yet once, at all events, he did a good turn. Before the introduction of paraffin oil into Scotland certain people from the lowlands to the east had the privilege of gathering torch fir from the forest of Glen More for lighting their homes. During these annual visits they quartered themselves upon the crofters of the glen and insisted on grazing their horses on the land. The natives longed to rid themselves of their unwelcome guests. Domhnall Mor determined to help the mortals of his glen. So one day, while the strangers were gathering torch fir in a remote part of the forest, they were startled to see a gigantic form, wonderfully clothed, suddenly appear before them. The giant fairy instantly attacked with sticks and stones so they fled in panic from the woods and never returned to Glen More.

CHS-25

Near Loch Morlich was the haunt of a more formidable spectre. The Bodach Lamh-dhearg – *Red-handed Spectre*. Lamh-dhearg was accustomed to challenge those who passed through his territory. There is an old undated account of this dreaded being in MacFarlane's *Geographical Collections*: 'A Spirit called Ly-Erg frequents Glen More. He appears with a red hand in the habit of a Souldier and challenges men to fight with him, as lately in 69 he fought with three Brothers one after another who immediately dyed thereafter.' I take it that 69 refers to the year 1669. Sir Walter Scott mentions the spectre in *Marmion*.

HOS-51

In a book by the Celtic scholar Alexander MacBain, the author gives two traditions to account for the disappearance of great areas of the old Caledonian Forest. The first tradition is that the Scottish Queen Mary was responsible. It is said that the Queen's husband, on his return home from abroad, on one occasion asked how his forests were [prospering] before he asked after her. When this came to the Queen's ears, she travelled north in anger and when she reached Kingussie (*Head of the Fir-wood*) she gave orders that preparations be made to set the woods alight. When all was ready she took her station on the top of Sron na Baruinn, *the Queen's Nose*, above Glen Feshie and there watched the forest go up in flames and smoke.

The second tradition is that the King of Norway was envious of the great woods of the Scottish Highlands. He sent his *muime* (nurse) to Scotland. Beginning in the north of Scotland she set the great forests afire. Since she had magic arts she kept herself aloft in the clouds while she rained down fire on the woods. She had devastated as far south as the Spey valley when a wise man of Badenoch hit upon a plan for destroying her and saving the remaining woods. He gathered together all the cattle over a wide area, the sheep and horses. He then separated the calves from the cows and the lambs from the sheep; the whinneying of mares separated from their foals added to the tumult.

The witch, enveloped in the dense cloud of smoke of her own making, heard the babel of sound. Her curiosity was such that she thrust her head out of the cloud. The Badenoch man was ready and had loaded his gun with a silver sixpence, and down came the witch at his feet. The forests of Rothiemurchus, Mar, and Ballochbuie were saved. But it seems likely that large areas of firs were burnt for the practical reason of ridding the district of the packs of wolves that roamed the great forest in early days.

HD-63

The River Feshie flows into the Spey near Loch Insh, Loch Innis – *Loch of the Island*. At the present time there is an island only when the loch is in flood, its site near where the Spey leaves the loch. In an old account of the district it is termed a 'half Yland.' The island, or peninsula, is high and wooded. A church is built on it and in the church is an ancient bronze bell which is said to be St Adamnan's. The mound on which the church stands is called sometimes Tom Eunan or Eonan, and Eonan is the name by which Adamnan is known in the Highlands (for example, Ard Eonaig by Loch Tay). Adamnan, celebrated for his *Life of St Columba*, was the ninth abbot of Hy (Iona). There is a legend that the bell was stolen and carried over the pass of Drumochter by the thieves. The theft was of no avail for the bell of itself returned over the hills and as it sped through the air is said to have intoned its name "Tom Eonan" for all to hear.

HOS-51

Let me mention the alternative name for Sgor an Lochan Uaine, a spur of Braeriach. Forty years ago I was told by the old Mar stalkers that Alexander Copeland, a keen mountaineer who sketched and published, if I remember rightly, the first panorama outline of the Cairngorm Range, had named it the Angel's Peak, in order, as he told my informants, to "keep the Devil's Point in its place." Twenty-five years later George MacPherson-Grant of the Ballindalloch family, who own Glen Feshie, told me that he used to hear the Glen Feshie stalkers refer to the hill as Sgor an Aingeil, the Gaelic translation of *Angel's Peak,* and he was greatly surprised to hear my account of the naming of the hill. Whatever its origin, the name Angel's Peak is now firmly established. There are innumerable Gaelic place-names which have now English equivalents, but this must be one of the very few English names to become Gaelicised. [Gaelic was more robust with names in the past and the Devil's Point, 'unbowlderised', is the Devil's Penis – and then there's the summit of Lochnager …]

HOS-51

SOUTH AND EAST

Craobh an Oir, *the Tree of Gold*, is a tall, weather-beaten tree, standing almost by itself on the heathery slope of Carn Crom on the north-west side of Glen Luibeg. It received its name centuries ago when MacKenzie of Dalmore (not far from Mar Lodge) hid treasure which he had taken from Lochaber raiders as they passed westward with booty stolen from the Lowlands. Tradition does not relate what that treasure was but it must have been valuable for Dalmore first hid it high in the Garbh Choire of Braeriach and then, feeling uneasy because it was so far away, brought it to the Tree of Gold. Some time later, hearing that the land in Cromar, thirty miles east of Mar, was to be sold and hoping to buy it, he dug up some of the gold and set out for Cromar. On reaching the high ground of Culblean, a hill near Morven, and looking down upon the expanse of loch, marsh and bog beneath him, he exclaimed, "God forbid that I should throw my gold beneath the waters" and abruptly returned to Mar. This time he buried the gold near the top of Carn Geldie and placed above it a great stone, on which was cut the figure of a horse-shoe. Traditionally, there it remains, waiting anyone fortunate enough to find it.

HD-63

A few miles west of Braemar, almost at the entrance to Mar Lodge, is an ancient pine tree which has a history dating back to the times when the clan spirit was all-powerful in the Highlands and when human life was held more cheaply. It was in the lifetime of Donald Farquharson, son of Fionnladh Mhor Mac Fhearachar, that the hanging of Lamond of Inverey took place at the gallows tree. Donald of Castleton, as he was called, must have lived and died between the sixteenth and seventeenth centuries, as his father, Fionnladh, fell at the battle of Pinkie, 1547. As a result of a raid on Deeside, Lord Huntly, desiring to punish the freebooters, called on the Farquharsons and Gordons of Abergeldie to apprehend and punish those responsible and, either rightly or wrongly, Lamond of Inverey was convicted – on the evidence of sheep found at his stronghold by the Ey. It is stated, however, by some that the sheep were placed there to inculpate him but 'so open was his guilt that no proof was needed and he was therefore led to a stout pine on a little knoll a short distance west of Mar Lodge Bridge and hanged on one of its branches.'

The following account is quoted from the well-known *Legends of the Braes o' Mar*, by one Grant who lived at Micras, opposite Abergeldie. The book was published in Aberdeen in 1861 and, although often unreliable, the story of the gallows tree as given in it is, in all probability, correct: 'His mother, a widow, followed the party that marched him off, praying them to save her only son but seeing that her tears availed nothing and considering the Clan Fionnladh responsible for his death she predicted the downfall of the clan in Gaelic rhyme, one verse of which went, translated, 'This tree will flourish high and broad/ Green as it grows to-day/ When from the banks of bonnie Dee/ Clan Fionnladh's all away.'

This prophecy is regarded as accomplished. Anyone will show you the dark doom's pine; but where are the Monaltries, flowers of chivalry; the Invereys, indomitable in war; the Auchendrynes, stout and true; the Balmorals, glorious and fleeting; the Allanaquoichs, ever worthy; and the Tullochcoys, heroes to the last? All and every one of them are gone. Invercauld became extinct in the male line and this is held to sufficiently fulfil the prophecy.

COH-21

The battle of the Cairnwell was fought in the year 1644. A body of men from Argyll, known as the Cleansers, ravaged the Highlands of Aberdeenshire that summer and one night 'lifted all the cattle from Glen Shee and Glen Isla'. The men, discovering their loss, made ready to attack the enemy, and in this fight a certain Braemar worthy known as the Cam Ruadh performed prodigies of valour and skill, shooting down the Cleansers one after the other with his arrow and turning what looked like a defeat into victory. But the Cam Ruadh towards the end of the fight was hit in the posterior by an arrow. The story is that when the Cam reached home his wife pulled out the arrow by standing on his back, one foot on either side of the arrow, and exerting all her strength; and that when the arrow had been removed the Cam celebrated the occasion by eating a large supper of venison!

Another legend of the Cairnwell is the killing of Captain Millar, the commander of the troops stationed in Braemar Castle. A strong man of Mar, known as Domhnall Dubh an t-Ephiteach, who the Braemar garrison had long endeavoured to capture –

he on one occasion stripped the sergeant of this clothing and sent him back to the castle without a stitch on him, hand tied behind his back and his clothes round his neck in a bundle – received word that Captain Millar and his wife were to cross the pass. Black Donald awaited his deadly enemy and shot and killed him, then accompanied his widow over the Cairnwell and, according to the legend, made himself so agreeable to the lady that before they had reached Glen Shee she asked him to marry her! The cairn of stones marking where Muckle Millar fell used to be pointed out but I doubt whether any person now alive knows where it is.

H&BC-48

Professor Watson has pointed out to me that Ath-fhinn, or A'an (Avon), means *Very Fair One*. This might well apply to the river itself, but the tradition, mentioned in the *Old Statistical Account*, is that Very Fair One was the name of the wife of Fingal, leader of the Fingalians, those supermen whose era is generally supposed to be the fourth century and whose deeds of prowess and daring are still remembered in the Highlands and in Eire. Fingal, or Fionn as he is usually spoken of, had one day been hunting, Ath-fhinn with him. When crossing the A'an at the end of the day, near the Linn at Inchrory, she slipped and was carried away by the swift stream. Two miles below the linn, at a place called Bogluachrach, her body was recovered and her grave is still pointed out. Fionn in his grief then spoke the following quatrain, set down in the *Old Statistical Account* [in Gaelic]: My wife has been drowned/ On the Fair Water of the slippery stone/ And since my wife has been drowned/ Let us call the river ATH-FHINN.

It is elsewhere noted that before the event the river had been called Uisge Ban, *Fair Water,* and that its name was then changed to Ath-fhinn, *Very Fair One.* The ford on the A'an below Loch A'an is to this day known at Ath nam Fiann, the *Ford of the Fingalians.*

HOS-51

BELTANE

Beltane falls on the first of May (old reckoning). Now little more than a name, yet in times gone by this was a solemn day when the world of the spirit was visualized by us mortals, when sacred verses were chanted in lonely places, when fairies in green dresses were seen.

The festival of Beltane dates back to far before the Christian era, observed by the Druids as a great festival in honour of the god Belus, and so Beltane is believed to be from *Beil-teine*, *the Fire of Belus*.

At Beltane fires were kindled on the hilltops and all the cattle of the district were driven through these fires in order to preserve them from harm until next May-day. On the day of Beltane the peat fire in every home was extinguished though it had burned continuously during the previous twelve months. After it had been put out it was rekindled from the *tein eigin*, the need-fire which had been lighted on the hill. In some districts the people as well as the cattle ran through the need-fires to purify them and safeguard them against mischance and illness during the year to come.

On the Day of Beltane the young generation sometimes wandered away to the moors and there made a round table in the heather. They cut a trench about the table, lit a great fire, and baked a great cake. This cake they cut into as many pieces as there were persons assembled. Charcoal was rubbed on one of the pieces of cake until it was black, the slices were then placed in a bonnet and each person, blindfold, took a slice. The person who drew the blackened portion was considered most unfortunate and, indeed, was in danger of being sacrificed to the god Belus. To avoid this fate he, or she, leaped six times over the flames of the fire.

Beltane or May Day was observed in all Celtic countries – Scotland, Ireland, Wales and the Isle of Man. When Queen Guinevere told her Knights of the Round

Table that she would go 'a-Maying' on the morrow she bade them be well horsed and dressed in green. Green is the fairy colour, which in the mystical ancient writings symbolized eternal youth and rebirth or resurrection. The earth each year is born again in green. The Initiate in the Ancient Mysteries was clothed in a robe of green to symbolize his own spiritual rebirth for on his initiation he had penetrated the Mystery of Death.

From the first day of November until Beltane the Fianna, the Celtic warrior heroes, were quartered on the people of the land but from Beltane to the beginning of November they were obliged to support themselves by fishing and hunting. The sun of a Beltan morning was believed to have great curative powers. The sick revived when placed in its rays. The tops of the hills were accordingly visited that morning in order to feel the earliest rays of the life-giving sun.

In Edinburgh there was, formerly, a great procession from the town at earliest dawn to view the sunrise from Arthur's Seat, a hill named after the idealistic King of the Round Table. When the traveller Pennant visited the Highlands in the eighteenth century he heard much of the festival of Beltane. He writes:

> The herdsmen of every village hold their Bel-tein, a rural sacrifice. They cut a square trench in the ground, leaving the turf in the middle. On that they make a fire of wood, on which they dress a large caudle [gruel] of eggs, butter, oatmeal and milk. They bring, besides the ingredients of the caudle, plenty of beer and whisky, for each of the company must contribute something. The rites begin with spilling some of the caudle on the ground, by way of libation. On that everyone takes a cake of oatmeal upon which are raised nine square knobs, each dedicated to some particular being, the supposed preserver of their flocks and herds, or to some particular animal, the real destroyer of them. Each person then turns his face to the fire, breaks off a knob, and flinging it over his shoulders say, "This I give to thee, preserve thou my horses; this to thee, preserve thou my sheep," and so on. After that they use the same ceremony to the noxious animals, "This I give to thee, O Fox, spare thou my lambs; this to thee, O Hooded Crow; this to thee, O Eagle."

IOW-33

EPILOGUE

SUNRISE ON CAIRNGORM

June; an hour before midnight Loch Morlich lay quiet and drowsy, the scent from the birches perfumed the night air, the sandpipers were quiet, the goosanders, their evening fishing over, were asleep. From afar came the hooting of an owl. Cairngorm rose clear and inviting. Although summer was here its snow-field Cuidhe Crom, remained broad and unbroken.

The track from Loch Morlich to Cairngorm leads first through the old pine forest then, at a height of 1,500 feet above the sea, leaves the trees and climbs through a land of stunted, wind-swept heather and rough hill grass. At midnight the sunset cast a strong light on this old path, the northern sky glowed and Venus was dimmed as she sank on the north-west horizon. Against this radiant sky rose Ben Wyvis, black as night and seeming close at hand. The west wind had fallen asleep, the air was windless, even the clouds were still. A meadow pipit fluttered from her nest beside the path, a cock grouse crowed with lusty surprise. The night wore on. Imperceptibly the afterglow travelled from north-west, through north, to north-east. Against the glowing sky was a bank of inky cloud, tenuous, motionless. At the zenith a star shone dimly.

I had climbed perhaps half-way up Cairngorm when, looking back, I saw an unexpected sight; against the mysterious afterglow came orange flashes of light – the distant lighthouse on Tarbat Ness sending its message not only out to sea but across the hills. The summer night was never dark yet this powerful light continued to be visible until sunrise was near. On a summer night the high hills are full of mystery. Like some cloud Cuidhe Crom seemed to float in air, Loch Morlich was a turquoise island amid a sea of pines, and across the twilight waters of the Moray Firth rose the cone of Morven in Caithness. Somewhere near me a ptarmigan, aroused from light sleep, croaked huskily.

Before two o'clock in the morning, sunset had merged into sunrise. Against that sunrise glow distant hills were so bright that one received the impression of fairy lights burning upon them yet, by looking back, one was greeted by the orange flashes of the Tarbat Ness light, rhythmic and powerful.

At two o'clock I reached the summit of Cairngorm. A faint air drifted across from the south but even here, more than four thousand feet above the sea, the night air was not cold. The sky, all but the northern fringe, was now overspread by thin, high cloud. In the light of dawn the snowy wastes of Ben MacDhui were pale and chill, across the distant Dee valley rose Lochnagar while Deeside's Morven, Ben Rinnes and the Buck o' the Cabrach all seemed near.

I lay on dry lichen and heather beside a snowfield at the source of a hill burn and there waited the strengthening of the day. The scene was one of outstanding beauty. The golden full moon had freed herself of cloud and as she sank toward the south-west horizon she shone warmly for a brief spell on the noble summit of Cairn Toul. Ptarmigan, awakening, called to the young day. The light strengthened and mysterious objects revealed themselves.

In this world of grandeur the sky was at rest, the hills were at rest, one had the impression of infinite peace, the material and the spiritual worlds had joined hands.

I walked by the ridge that bounds the two fine corries of Coire Cas (*Steep Corrie*) and Coire an t-Sneachda (*Snowy Corrie*) to the spur at Cairn Lochan and as I walked it was curious to see grey twilight to the south while the sunrise glow burned faintly on the north-facing slopes.

The actual rising of the sun came at a few minutes after four o'clock by summer time. Red, benign, enormous, and quivering, he climbed from the sea off the Banff-shire coast and seemed to hold friendly converse with the moon that hung golden above the soft snows of Cairn Toul. I looked into the abyss of Coire an Lochain and saw the track of a recent avalanche; great blocks of snow lay on the gentle slopes between precipice and lochan.

South of Cairn Lochan lies one of the highest tarns in Scotland, Lochan Buidhe, 3,700 feet. The way from Cairn Lochan to Lochan Buidhe lies across pleasant grassy slopes where the flowers of the cushion pink blend with the green leaves of the tiny Alpine willow. In the silence of that early morning Lochan Buidhe lay as though entranced. Midsummer had come yet a snowfield still gripped it south shore and, even as I watched, delicate fingers of new-formed ice stealthily felt their way across the calm waters.

Old withered grass, bent and flattened towards the north-east, showed the track of the autumn south-west gales that had preceded the snows of winter. Although the sun was risen he was hidden by a bank of cloud which lay close to the horizon and the air was now colder than at any time during the night.

Then the sun gradually climbed above the clouds and the slopes of Brae Riach across Lairig Ghru were lighted up. Looking away beyond the Lairig I saw the far-distant hills on the north-west seaboard. They appeared to be held without support in the blue sky, their snowfields radiant and ethereal.

No pen could describe the beauty of the early morning – a beauty that was dream-like and soul-stirring. There was nothing austere about the Cairngorms today, smilingly they greeted a perfect summer morning, smilingly and patiently they awaited the life-giving power of the sun. On the slopes of Ben MacDhui the snow was hard, frost diamonds glistened on its surface. High overhead sped a dotterel. An old ptarmigan, dozing behind a stone, bestirred himself and he and his lady ran unwillingly from the unexpected visitor.

The sun gained power. It shone warmly beside Lochan Buidhe and I lay down upon a dry grassy bank and sank into deep dreamless sleep. From time to time for a few seconds I awoke and noted with each awakening the increased brilliance of the light. Two hours later I awoke finally into a different world and rose to my feet. Gone were the half lights, gone was plum-coloured Ben Rinnes, gone the young ice on Lochan Buidhe, gone were the diamonds of frost on the snow-fields. The hills were now in brilliant sun flood, high in an azure sky billowy clouds floated majestically, the snow-fields gleamed (the eye could scarce rest upon them), on the warm breeze was the scent of blaeberry and crowberry, no longer did the distant hills appear magically raised in air but now rose firmly planted on the earth, and the snowy corries of Ben Nevis to the west became once more strong and abiding.

The hills were awake; gone the season of dreams.

IOW-33

Seton Gordon looking at a Scots fir seedling on Carn a' Mhaim

AFTERWORD

WALKING WITH SETON GORDON

The Black Wood, Rannoch

The wood is lit like a dream: the peripheries smoke in a bright mist. I enter it at Carie and start to walk south-west up the slope away from the loch. I gain some height and then turn west along a track through pines frosted in lichen. It is the faintest of paths, sometimes just a dent in the moss where deer have passed.

I am heading for the Dall burn which marks the eastern boundary of the Black Wood, a fragment of old pine forest that hangs below the south shore of Loch Rannoch like the keel of a boat. The wood is a remnant of the pine forest that swept across much of the Highlands over 5,000 years ago. Only a few pockets of the forest remain, like dark sun-spots on the map. But the roots and stumps of this great sea of pines are still preserved in the peat bogs that spread and smothered these northern pinewoods as the climate moistened and warmed. These ancient roots appear along the beaches where storms have woken them and they emerge from the peat bogs like splinters working themselves free from skin. They lodge in the land like broken harpoon tips inside a whale.

I pause to examine the lichen that seems to cover every branch and twig. It is pale turquoise resembling verdigris and gives off a delicate light so the trees glow very faintly. I pick a handful of lichen and hold it up to my nose. It smells of leaf litter but the smell is drier and less earthy. It is the trace of a scent, like an old spoor.

There is someone I have followed into the wood. Seventy years ago the writer and naturalist Seton Gordon drove his car west from Loch Tummel dropping down to the village of Kinloch Rannoch. It was late September 1938. That morning Gordon wrote, 'a thin cap of mist clothed the summit of Schiehallion and as the mist rose and fell it showed at times a faint golden gleam as the sun lit up the fringes of the cloud'. In Munich the major European powers were gathering to discuss the annexation of the Sudetenland to Germany. Gordon remarks that it was 'a time of the most tense international crisis, and the air was heavy with forebodings'. In the village he passed a police car distributing gas masks, the constables talking quietly to one another 'as though they could scarcely credit this menace of imminent war'. Gordon left Kinloch Rannoch and crossed the river Tummel, travelling west along the south shore of the loch towards the Black Wood. He later wrote that, entering the Black Wood that day, he 'forgot for a time the evil days through which Europe was passing in the strength and beauty of the old pines'.

For some weeks I had been reading about the Black Wood with the map spread out like a picnic rug over the floor. I discovered it held at least 150 types of lichen, that there were pine martin, red squirrel, black grouse, crossbill; as well as pine there were silver and downy birch, juniper, alder, rowan, aspen and willow. It seemed such a rich and fascinating habitat. But what drew me most to the wood was reading that simple, dignified phrase of Gordon's: 'in the strength and beauty of the old pines'. It was a phrase that had a resonance, an echo that kept sounding in me. I wanted very much to walk amongst those trees, to experience their beauty. So the Black Wood fixed itself in my mind and started to draw me in. Seton Gordon would be my guide.

I am making slow progress towards the Dall. The path has dried up and the trees are thicker here. Clumps of spruce send me swerving like a hare to find a way through. I look for seams of light through the trees like a boat scanning for navigable leads in sea ice.

Seton Gordon published twenty-seven books over a long life spent studying and photographing the wildlife of the Scottish Highlands. Many of his photographs are remarkable, born from cumbersome cameras; he took his first photograph of an eagle in 1904 when he was 18. His photographs of eagles on their nest published in *Days With the Golden Eagle* (1927) and *The Golden Eagle: King of Birds* (1955) are extraordinary for their intimacy and clarity. In a photograph taken in 1922 a parent bird lands on the nest with a grouse in its talons as a cloud of flies spits out from an old carcass on the eyrie, as if the landing eagle has set off an explosion there. Another beautiful photograph shows a pair of Greenshank changing places on their nest. As one bird rises from the eggs you see the dappled pattern of the shells matches the bird's breast.

Many writers and naturalists have been inspired by Gordon's work and followed him into the woods and hills. Above all he was an exemplary field naturalist. Attentive is the word I think of. That lovely verb: 'attend', to turn one's ear to; to look after; to care for; to be in mind; to wait upon … Once, during a heat wave, Gordon scooped a snowball from high in the Cairngorms to cool the panting of a nesting dotterel. He stood behind the bird holding the snowball like a moon till she closed her bill and dozed in the grateful cold.

The writer Barry Lopez observed in his work about the history and natural history of the Arctic, *Arctic Dreams*, that 'It is easy to underestimate the power of a long-term association with the land, not just with a specific spot but with the span of it in memory and imagination, how it fills, for example, one's dreams.' Seton Gordon's work is like this. What Gordon sees in the land is a place suffused with memories, stories, myths … the entire span of it. During his visit to the Black Wood, Gordon found a pine at the edge of the loch that had been sawn off near its base. He describes how 'out of curiosity' he began to count its rings: it had lived 214 years. Only a little further along the loch side he is tacking again to the small burial ground of St Michaels to explore the large stone there and recount its gruesome history. He spies the smallest hill burns as a robin might a worm, and untangles the meaning of their Gaelic names. Over on the north shore of the loch he has suddenly spied *Caochan na Fala*, the streamlet of blood, and proceeds to tell us the story of the fifteenth century clan skirmish there that gave the burn its name.

In *Arctic Dreams* Lopez writes that 'the Eskimo travels somewhat like the arctic fox, turning aside to investigate something unusual.' This is how Gordon writes, twisting through the history of a place, doubling back on himself to investigate an alpine plant, a summer snow-field, to count the rings of a fallen tree.

I reach the Dall burn and cross on the forestry bridge. The trees here are all forestry plantation with the occasional solitary pine, relics from the old wood. They loom out of the mist like great beasts grazing amongst the smaller trees. Their bark is fissured and gnarled like an elephant's skin. Crossing the burn I start to drop north along a muddy track back towards the loch. I pass stacks of timber piled up on either side of the path. The trees are stacked in the shape of an upturned boat like a great ark. It's as if the loch had suddenly drained and left this giant boat stranded on the high ground.

West of the Dall the forestry starts to give way to the old wood. It is a movement into a different stratum, a fading through shades as birches begin to dilute the lines of spruces. Heather and blaeberry bushes grow beneath the trees and the huge pines wade amongst them. It is a movement too into a more breathable space; the wood here does not choke the light. As Gordon observed about the Black Wood: 'in these natural-grown pine forests the trees do not grow so densely as to destroy the lesser vegetation, and the heather this day of late September, was purple beneath the old pines.'

Seton Gordon can strike a lonely figure. As the great authority on Gordon's work Hamish Brown points out, for the first three decades of the twentieth century Gordon was the only full-time practising naturalist in Britain. This at a time when attitudes to Britain's wildlife, and in particular its birds of prey, ranged from the callous to the brutal. As the writer Jim Crumley (who has also walked with Gordon's ghost) notes, Gordon stood apart as someone who looked at eagles 'through camera and telescope rather than along the barrel of a shotgun'. Gordon was a pioneer: he observed behaviour in eagles that no one else had recorded. His work, to quote from Lopez once more: 'pried the landscape loose from its anonymity'. But it was work that was borne by him adrift of prevailing attitudes. The acknowledged authority of birds of prey Leslie Brown reminds us that even the 1954 Bird Preservation Act had not the slightest effect in checking the abuse of golden eagles in Scotland. It is interesting to note that in 1946 Gordon along with the respected naturalist Frank Fraser Darling argued against a proposal to survey the eagle population. Their point was that ignorance on the subject was beneficial to the conservation of the birds, that any figures would simply fuel a call to reduce the population. Leslie Brown estimated in the 1970s that 80–90 pairs of golden eagles were destroyed or failed to breed every year throughout Scotland. Brown proportioned this as 'forty pairs deliberately destroyed or disturbed by gamekeepers and shepherds; about thirty due to casual or unintentional human interference; and the rest to egg collectors and natural losses'. In the last decade of his life Gordon would have also been aware that the use of Dieldrin in sheep dips in the 1970s was dramatically reducing the breeding success of eagles in the West Highlands. The roll call of eagles trapped, poisoned and shot on his watch must have cut Gordon very deeply. When he published one of his most admired books *The Cairngorm Hills of Scotland* in 1925 he notes that the wildcat, raven, polecat and kite had vanished from those hills. Gordon was born at the end of a century in which golden eagles, wildcats and pine martins where bagged as vermin in Victorian game books. He turned 32 the year the last white tailed eagle was shot in Scotland in 1918. Two years earlier the last known pair of ospreys bred on Loch Loyne. Starting work as a naturalist with that bleak legacy, Gordon can seem like a lonely custodian of the wild places, a figure as isolated as the old kite's nest he describes in the Cairngorm woods: 'Another bird which the old trees must have known in their youth was the kite. It is now sixty years since the kite nested in the pine forests of the Cairngorms but one of the nests remains where it was built, in the fork of an old Scots fir.'

But even as he is cataloguing those species that have been driven out of the Cairngorms he is reminding us that 'the golden eagle, fox, and falcon remain'. Above all the eagle, a bird he draws and redraws in his photographs and observations, as if to etch its survival into us:

> *When, for a minute, the storm lessened I saw the eagle perched on the hill-top opposite. On a knife-like ridge the great bird stood, seemingly indifferent to the bitter wind, then, as I watched, she (it was the hen bird) sprang*

magnificently into space and mounted on her broad wings on the frosty breeze.'

—Days With the Golden Eagle

When Gordon left the Black Wood that day in 1938, he drove west along the shore road and called at a small post office. He paused here a while and listened in with the postmistress on the wireless to the launch of the *Queen Elizabeth*. I have stopped to rest in the heart of the old wood and find myself drawn to that image of the huge ship sliding from its berth and calving into the dock. In front of me are the remains of old canals dug in the nineteenth century to float timber out of the wood into Loch Rannoch. The canals are long filled in and are covered in mosses, ferns and liverworts. They look like green bobsleigh runs winding away through the trees. I think of how those great pines must have crashed into the loch below, the tremendous displacement of water before they righted into buoyancy, the same movement Gordon would have heard as he listened to the launch of the ship.

I sit down beside the old canal. My eye is drawn again to the lichens. I reach across to touch some growing on the bark of a pine. It is tougher than it looks and feels like worn dead skin. I try to trace the different patterns: snow crystals; down feathers; a crow's feet crease on someone's face; knuckle dents; a map of river tributaries.

The timber that floated down these canals was destined for building projects in towns like Perth and Dundee that were expanding to the east. The idea was that the timber would be floated to the foot of Loch Rannoch and then down the river Tummel and out into the estuary of the Tay. Much of the timber never made it that far, snagging in rapids along the river, clogging the waterways, as if reversing the salmon's precarious journey to its spawning grounds.

The canal scheme failed but timber continued to be taken from the Black Wood. War increased the demand and Gordon laments in a single brief footnote: 'As I revise this chapter (1942) many of the finest trees have been felled in the Black Wood.' In 1947 the wood was purchased by the Forestry Commission, deer were brought under control and the young trees were able to establish. It became a protected Forest Reserve in 1975. The wood was attended to.

Not far from where Gordon must have stooped to age that felled tree, I stop to explore a huge pine. Its bark plates the trunk in wedges as thick as my arm. Dead pine needles stick to the bark caught in cobwebs that cover its cracks and gullies. The bark flakes easily when you touch it. The webs seem to be holding the bark in place like a hairnet. Lying down at the foot of the tree I tilt my head back and gaze up the length of the trunk. It looks like a dried river bed, a parched and cracked landscape.

I continue to drop slowly north-west towards the loch shore. The black pines are tinted with red along the joins of the bark and where it has flaked off like sunburnt skin. Around the pines the slender birches bend and lean to one another like a room of people. I walk back along the shore road at dusk. Woodcock spring away from me out of the reedy verge. One is so close that I can see its long beak, ashen like the pale birches at its base, bright black at the tip as if it had been dipped in ink. The rusty brown rump of its tail is the same colour as the reds that tint the pine bark.

Before I left the wood I came across a pine with a rowan clinging to it. The silver trunk of the rowan was strapped to the dark pine like an aqualung. I realise I have not so much been following him as been borne by Gordon through the Black Wood today. I have leaned on him.

There is a book that I would love to have lent Seton Gordon. He may have even read it, but I can't be sure. Published in 1967, J.A. Baker's masterpiece *The Peregrine* is an extraordinary evocation of the spirit of the peregrine falcon and of the author's ceaseless questing after the bird. I think Gordon would have admired and recognised Baker's reverence for the peregrine and his ability to bind the bird and its landscape together. One sentence in Baker's book rings out sharp as a peregrine against a blue winter sky: 'The hardest thing of all to see is what is really there'. For Baker, pictures of birds of prey in books are 'waxworks beside the passionate mobility of the living bird'. To my mind, Seton Gordon's photographs capture that passionate mobility: they are never waxworks. To borrow a phrase from Seamus Heaney, when I first saw Gordon's photographs of eagles their 'wildness tore through me'. Gordon's writing and photographs always strive after what is really there.

Once, after listening to the song of a Greenshank, Gordon found, like a Highland Orpheus, he could reproduce the bird's song on his bagpipe chanter. Returning again and again to his books, his photographs, to the paths he trod through the hills and woods, I pick out Seton Gordon's own particular song and find it still resonating.

James Macdonald Lockhart

BIBLIOGRAPHY TO THE AFTERWORD

Baker, J.A. – *The Peregrine* (Collins, 1967)

Crumley, Jim – *Among Mountains* (Mainstream, 1993)

Brown, Hamish – *Seton Gordon's Scotland: An Anthology* (Whittles Publishing, 2005)

Brown, Leslie – *British Birds of Prey* (Collins, 1976)

Gordon, Seton – *The Cairngorm Hills of Scotland* (Cassell, 1925)

Gordon, Seton – *Highways & Byways in the Central Highlands* (Macmillan, 1949)

Gordon, Seton – *In Search of Northern Birds* (Eyre & Spottiswoode, 1942)

Gordon, Seton – *Days With the Golden Eagle* [Introduction by Jim Crumley] (Whittles Publishing, 2003)

Gordon, Seton – *The Golden Eagle: King of Birds* (Collins, 1955)

Heaney, Seamus – *Seeing Things* (Faber, 1991)

Lopez, Barry - *Arctic Dreams: Imagination and Desire in a Northern Landscape* (Harvill, 1999)

Macfarlane, Robert – *The Wild Places* (Granta, 2007)

Steel, Pamela & Macdonald, Sarah – *The Singing Forest* (Loch Cottage, 2004)

Seton Gordon's Scotland:
an anthology

Hamish Brown

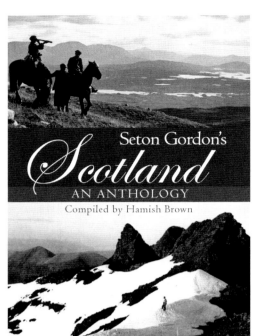

Available for the first time, a selection of Seton Gordon's writing, skilfully and intuitively anthologised

Seton Gordon was only a boy when he began exploring the Cairngorms, fascinated by its wildlife and seeking to photograph all he saw – he later became a pioneer naturalist, photographer and folklorist. He wrote about the land that is ScotLAND, her flora and fauna, her people, her spirits, her often violent past. He took the earliest pictures of golden eagles at their eyries and throughout the first half of the 20th century came to know Scotland's remotest corners, amassing a unique photographic record, recording the changing social life of the islands, collecting a mass of folklore and historical stories, lecturing and writing both for regular publications and in 27 books.

Welcomed in croft or palace, a keen piper, inevitably dressed in kilt and bunnet, Seton Gordon was one of the age's great characters.

This selection from his writings gives a fascinating insight of the man and his great versatility. Hamish Brown, himself a Scottish outdoors enthusiast and well-known author, has been a lifelong admirer of Seton Gordon and his books, and has created a book to treasure.

'...it is a kaleidoscope of a way of life in the first half of the 20th century, a contribution of great importance, ...an utterly fascinating book'. *Highland News*

'...thoroughly readable, a gem of a book. It captures the spirit of the man ... and is packed with information and anecdote'. *Loose Scree*

'This is a very special book; a real celebration of the writings of that most influential and kindly of Highland gentlemen... Hamish has done Seton's works and memory proud...' *Scottish Mountaineering Club Journal*

'... This fine book presents a wonderful selection, ranging from powerfully descriptive passages, beautiful descriptions of birds and other wildlife, to myths and legends and the lives of the peoples of the Highlands and Islands...' *BIRDS*

Contents: The Cairngorms; The Length of the Land; The Outer Hebrides; Ways That Are Gone; Birds Above All; Hill Days; Western Isles; The Unrestful Past; Bird Notes; A Vanished World; Epilogue

ISBN 978-1904445-73-9   240 × 170 mm   352pp   illustrated with original photographs   softback   £19.99

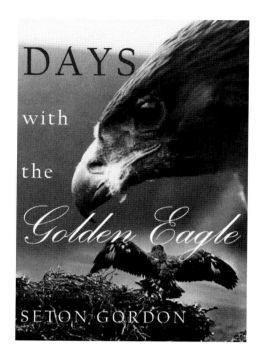

DAYS with the
Golden Eagle

Seton Gordon

A reprint of the classic eagle book and one of the most acclaimed of Seton Gordon's 27 books

Seton Gordon was among the first to observe in detail – through countless hours in his hide – the daily life of this magnificent bird and to present in his books an account of their habitat, diet and behaviour. From life day to day on the eyrie, through the different Scottish landscapes and the interaction of the eagles with other wildlife – it is all covered, and all in his inimitable style:

The eagle as she broods on her eyrie in this country of wild primeval forest has an inspiring view. She looks across to the high tops and sees the early morning sun flood the snowy slopes with rosy light. She hears from the forest below her the soft bubbling notes of the amorous blackcock at their fighting-ground, and the wild clarion call of the missel-thrush as he greets the April dawn. Other sounds she hears: the hoarse bark of a hind, the curious sneezing cry of a capercaillie on some pine tree, the distant melody of curlew and golden plover on the brown moorland, the becking of a cock grouse as he shakes the frosty dew from his plumage. I remember once spending a night beside an eagle at the eyrie and seeing the first sun-flush burn upon her golden head, so that it was no longer golden but deep rose coloured; and so I like to picture that lonely eyrie on many calm, sunny days when spring is young and when all the life of the lonely upland places is commencing slowly to stir to the increasing power of the sun.

'Days with the Golden Eagle *is a book that fully deserves a reprint. ...The author and his books were an inspiration to me and countless others who have been transported by his descriptive writing into Scotland's wild lands, to witness, often in close detail, the home life of our most spectacular raptor. The true value of this book is that it introduces new generations of readers not only to the Golden Eagle and its home but also to the other creatures that share these special places. ...Readers will surely be encouraged to tread the hills, seek the secrets, and feel the magic. Maybe even more important the book will instil a love of nature that bestows a strong feeling of guardianship for all wildlife that lives in these remote areas. ...Seton Gordon died in 1977 but I am sure for as long as eagles fly his books will be avidly read.'* John Muir Trust Journal

'[Days of the Golden Eagle] *will bring one of the best nature writers in Scotland to a new audience. Whilst the text is in many ways as fresh and stimulating as the day it was written, the photographs are equally outstanding. ...the close-up of the head and upper neck of the juvenile golden eagle on the front cover and the frontispiece has a haunting quality that seems to imprint on the mind...The text is sometimes unbelievable in its impact such as the lines,* There was no breeze in the old pine forest, and the ancient, heavy crowned trees seemed to hold their green branches eagerly towards the strong sunlight. *Who writes like this these days and who has that depth of feeling that comes out in the lines so often it is almost mesmerising? Much of what the author describes is still there but perhaps we do not look in the same way any more.'* Highland News

ISBN 978-1870325-35-6   240 × 170 mm   192pp   illustrated   softback   £16.95

The Mountains Look on Marrakech

A trek along the Atlas Mountains

Hamish Brown

A visual and literary feast of travel writing from an expert

After an initial visit of three months to the Atlas Mountains in 1965, well-known travel writer, climber and photographer Hamish Brown has been back every year since, and this book is something of a love story about one man's lifelong devotion to the Atlas Mountains and the Berber Highlanders who so strongly remind him of Scottish history, although in a harsher, bigger world where storms and flash floods can cause havoc.

In his own words, 'I had put feet to my dream and this book is the story of that dream, the end-to-end trek of the Atlas Mountains, a 900-mile walk in 96 days, which I want to share before everything recedes like a tide into the flat waters of memory.'

Hamish makes light of what was a complicated and notable journey with endless passes, gorges and peaks taken in. With his wide knowledge of the Atlas and careful planning, the journey was kept in steady flow despite the many hazards, but it is the many cameos of description, meetings with villagers, entertaining folk tales and much more that will beguile the reader and make this one of the classic stories of modern adventuring.

As a companion on our literary journey the author is an expert guide. ... His observations are couched in picturesque vocabulary or have a freshness of expression that delights. ...will doubtless become compulsory reading. **Loose Scree**

The book is a delight. Much more than a mere travelogue, the journey is the thread along which the narrative is woven. ...a good read for armchair travellers. ***John Muir Trust Journal***

This outstanding travelogue is complemented by superb images. ***The Scots Magazine***

ISBN 978-1870325-29-5   240 × 170mm   304pp incl. 16pp colour section hardback   £25

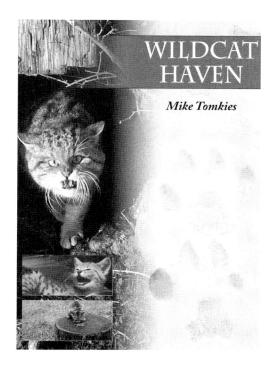

WILDCAT HAVEN

Mike Tomkies

A new edition of the first authoritative account about wildcats

Some seven years after abandoning the life of an international journalist for a life in the wilds, *Mike Tomkies* began a remarkable experiment, rearing the most ferocious animal to roam wild in Britain – the Scottish wildcat.

The true wildcat is now an endangered species and only to be found in inaccessible parts of the Scottish mountains. It may look like a giant domestic tabby, but with its bright red tongue and vicious claws, it is a formidable and fearless opponent of mankind. It is justly noted for being untameable.

Mike became the custodian of two spitfire kittens, found abandoned in a ditch when only a few weeks old. Even before they were fully weaned in his kitchen, they could be approached only with extreme care, usually with thick gauntlets as protection against the ravages of tooth and claw. He named them Cleo and Patra. The kittens were only seven months old when a spitting and snarling ten-year-old tomcat arrived from the London Zoo to change all their lives …

Mike resolved to breed a wildcat family and prepare them for a return to the wild. His extraordinary adventures in raising and releasing no fewer than three litters, two pure wildcat and one a hybrid from a domestic male gone wild, are full of incident, at times hilarious, and deeply moving. The runt of Cleo's second litter demolished Mike's last defences by giving him her total trust and affection while fiercely retaining an utterly wild and independent nature. So, he became the first to 'tame' a wildcat.

Little of the scant scientific theory on wildcat behaviour was borne out by his careful observations. This unique story of communion between man and animal is taken from two books that have long been out of print – *My Wilderness Wildcats* and *Liane, A Cat from the Wild* – revised and updated by the author and illustrated with many new photographs, all in colour. An update of the lengthy appendix which discusses wildcat populations, history and research on the breed including issues of genetic purity is included in this new edition.

About the author: Mike Tomkies is a well-known naturalist, writer and film-maker and has lived for 35 years in remote and wild places in the Scottish Highlands, Canada and Spain. He is an Honorary Fellow of the Royal Zoological Society of Scotland. His other books include *Moobli, Alone in the Wilderness, Between Earth and Paradise, Out of the Wild, Golden Eagle Years, On Wing and Wild Water, My Wicked First Life—before the wilderness, Rare, Wild and Free* and *Backwoods Mates to Hollywood's Greats*.

ISBN 978-1904445-75-3   240 × 170mm   softback   192pp + 24pp colour section   £18.99

To order any of these titles contact:
Whittles Publishing, Dunbeath, Caithness, Scotland. KW6 6EY, UK
T: +44(0)1593-731 333; F: +44(0)1593-731 400
Email: info@whittlespublishing.com • www.whittlespublishing.com